£MPATHI$ING WITH THE £GO OF THE £NTR€PR€N€UR

ROBERT FRITH

ROBERT FRITH PUBLISHING

EMPATHISING WITH THE EGO OF THE ENTREPRENEUR

First published in 2014 by Robert Frith Publishing

Designed by Loulita Gill Design, Bristol
Edited by Kate Gilchrist, London
Photograph by SMS Creative Photography, Oxted

British Library Cataloguing in Publication Data
A catalogue record of this book is available from the British Library

ISBN 978-0-9927951-0-8

I am dedicating this book to everyone I have met in
my personal and business life - so far.
Particularly those who have made me laugh
and especially those who have given me short putts.

CONTENTS

CHAPTER ONE

THIS IS THE KEY FOR THE IGNITION

1.1 What has made you successful?

So you want to become an entrepreneur? There would be little point if you didn't want to be successful as well. Otherwise why not continue with your day job?

What makes you able to be an entrepreneur and what will make you successful?

Success, as you shall read, is mainly measured in terms of financial success. That is entirely understandable in today's material world. Albeit the successful entrepreneur, while they like the trappings of success often want more and more, and then often wish to hide their gains. Why when they worked so hard?

But the leading question and the fundamental issue of this book is what is in the make-up of an entrepreneur?

They will take risks today for the potential benefits tomorrow. Not everyone can do it, even though they may think they can. And even fewer are successful.

To produce this book we conducted a survey (see Chapter 9). One of the free format questions was:

£££ OUR SURVEY ASKED:

What has made you successful?

And among many replies, sample answers were:

- Hard work
- Drive, hard work and attentiveness to servicing customers
- Luck, seeing the opportunity and working hard
- Sheer hard work
- Persistence and determination
- Adaptability and sheer hard work
- Total dedication
- Will to win and succeed
- Determination
- Vision, determination and the ability to develop relationships
- DNA and experience in early years

There are some very clear themes here. Let's take three of them as a taster for the rest of the book.

Firstly, 'Hard work' is mentioned in almost all of these answers, but what does that mean? Does it mean sacrificing long hours at work and as a result giving up other activities or family life to go that extra mile to ensure complete satisfaction for your customers? Is that meant to be hard work?

£££ OUR SURVEY ASKED:

Do you spend more time than you feel you should on the business?

A: 36% said yes

£££ OUR SURVEY ASKED:

Do you feel that you do not have a work/life balance?

A: 44% agreed

These numbers are higher than those that would be provided by salaried staff.

Secondly, 'Luck': please discuss at your next dinner party, or in the pub or restaurant with your friends what luck really means.

£££ OUR SURVEY ASKED:
Do you think you have had some luck?
A: 96% said yes

£££ OUR SURVEY ASKED:
If so, mark its importance to where you are now, out of 10
A: This scored 7.29 out of 10!

What makes you lucky? If that is a prerequisite of being an entrepreneur, why bother if it is all simply reliant on the roll of a dice?

Thirdly 'Vision': who has vision, who can predict the future? Do you need to be an astrologer to predict that a product has a market and will sell? How ridiculous, but do successful entrepreneurs possess this skill.

£££ OUR SURVEY ASKED:
Do you have an overall strategy?
A: 84% said yes

£££ OUR SURVEY ASKED:
If so how important is it to keep to it, out of 10
A: This scored 8.1 out of 10

Entrepreneurs may have a strategy, but adaptability and flexibility are also key attributes.

And yet, over time and in the future, many people will start businesses and be successful and they will come up with the same formula. 'I worked hard', 'I was lucky because….' 'I had a strategy and could see the market for this product'.

Why can't you do the same? Perhaps you have, but why can't everyone?

Also importantly what criteria have **not** been mentioned in these answers?

For example:

- 'I took risks and as a result became successful', how?

- 'Luckily the recession was over (or the competition had gone bankrupt) so success came my way', how?

- 'I was backed with enough seed capital', how?

- And most importantly, I knew I had ALL the skills to be a successful entrepreneur.

'DNA and experience in early years' was an unsolicited answer provided by a highly successful entrepreneur, what did he mean?

That is what this book is about.

So do you 'have it', 'have what it takes', or 'have the constituent parts in your make up'?

The conclusion in Chapter 9.3, which sets out the major characteristics of an entrepreneur, may surprise you. Entrepreneurs will recognise part, or all, of themselves.

1.2 The choice of title

The title of the book is 'Empathising with the ego of the entrepreneur' and it was chosen for very good reasons.

There were a number of options for the title of this book which all ran a close second, but when it came down to the final choice, there was a clear winner.

The entrepreneur is a noteworthy person in our society. They are generally well-respected, admired and considered to be important people. They can be the butt of jokes, the cause of jealousy and, at times, considered arrogant because they have what we don't have – money and the ability to make choices. However, despite the wealth they may (and 'may' is the operative word here) create for themselves – they also create wealth for others. This wealth can take the form of jobs, opportunities and a contribution to the state in taxes.

So is it unfair to be too judgemental and consider entrepreneurs to be selfish, arrogant and just "out for themselves"? Many others around them clearly benefit, as well.

Also, the entrepreneur is, by default, an interesting person, who engages with other interesting people, is generally full of ideas and often has a different approach, aspect and alternative view on life. They are 'alternative' in many respects to the average person and it is extremely important, therefore, to be able to empathise with the entrepreneur, and of course, for the entrepreneur to empathise with the average person. It is a two-way street and hopefully this book goes a long way in explaining that and completing everyone's understanding.

The entrepreneur, as with everyone, has an ego and clearly, again, this is different to other people. Ego is defined later in this book and is not meant in any way to be a derogatory term, but describes the passionate, driven and focused individual, who is the ENTREPRENEUR.

The other titles for the book which were considered were:

1. **The Entrepreneur's DNA**

   This gives an insight into some of what will be covered throughout the book. However, this would concentrate only on the internal workings of the entrepreneur.

   It is necessary to also include what actually makes them tick and ask why they do operate the way they do? The important areas to address and comprehend are how others should react to, and with, entrepreneurs. How to deal with them, understand them and cope with their high energy levels, are as important as understanding why the entrepreneur could be considered a loner, or individualistic at best.

Entrepreneurs can come across as being self-centred and as mentioned above "out for themselves" but hopefully, as you read on, that will be dispelled.

Their 'DNA' or internal make-up is very different to the employees they need to help create their business, and their 'DNA' is obviously opposite to the public service worker who provides them with services that we all use and enjoy, in respect of health, education and policing. Do entrepreneurs understand such people? Do entrepreneurs think that throwing their money, thoughts and charisma at a problem solves it?

So 'DNA' is important but it is not the entire picture. This title gives the impression that we are looking at the internal workings and 'engine' in too much detail. So it is unsatisfactory and limited.

2. Managing for the New Century in the Entrepreneurs' World

Yes, this could be a good title, but it would indicate a book on management and a tool for those who manage for, with and alongside the entrepreneur.

It would purely consider the entrepreneur's perspective, to be used by those that operate in the entrepreneur's world, but it, in itself, would not explain the mind of the entrepreneur.

So, just as the previous title would explain the inner workings of an entrepreneur, this title would only explain the external interactions of an entrepreneur. Both are vitally important, so the title is, like the previous one, inappropriate.

3. The Psychology of Profit

This title may seem to fit both the internal and external workings, however, not every entrepreneur runs a profitable organisation, nor is successful.

So while the book would deal with the psychology, the profit is still up for debate. It is a nice title for management gurus and trainers, and it would be useful if someone wrote a book or management manual on this subject.

Reference to this book would be essential for the above titles. It is not often that a writer offers their own book as reference, but there you go. The ego of a writer can be the same as any entrepreneur as the creativity involved in writing a book is the same as an invention, business idea, business or venture. It needs inception, delivery and marketing.

This title does not cover interaction with others and again is therefore incomplete and inapplicable.

Empathising with the Ego of the Entrepreneur

So now it is imperative to explain the meaning of this book's title so you understand the angle from which this book is written and hopefully enjoy it more and appreciate it to its fullest.

To explain the choice of words in the title:

Empathising

The dictionary definition is: "Empathy is the capacity to recognise feelings that are being experienced by another sentient or fictional being. Someone may need to have a certain amount of empathy before they are able to feel compassion."

This word was chosen to demonstrate that the entrepreneur is not a foreign body from foreign parts or outer space. They are human and have to get along with themselves before being able to ably communicate with those around them.

Entrepreneurs have feelings. They, despite most reactions, are human and a human with special skills. So we all need to relate to that person. There is an overriding need for those around to show understanding, to relate and to meet with the mind of our entrepreneur. Those who work for an entrepreneur will often become frustrated by their overarching demands and excessive energy and passion. However, they should soon realise that the end game makes everyone a winner.

Their will to succeed and passion can be passed on to employees and make a successful operation.

With the Ego

For your information: "Ego is the Latin word for 'I', often used to mean self".

Everyone has an ego, it depends on how strongly they show this ego as to whether it is noticed or not.

The entrepreneur has to get things done. They are recognised as being an achiever and therefore frequently demonstrate an ego.

Once famous, though, the ego is then on display for everyone to see. The entrepreneur when they become famous will show their ego for all it's worth. The media likes to report on the entrepreneur and in particular their failures and mistakes. It is widely recognised that this sells papers.

The entrepreneur does not necessarily set out to be famous but if they manage to establish a large organisation or a well-known brand, or sell out for a large sum of money, then they will attract fame. Fame will give them adulation which they can seek. Not a bad thing, but often they do not seek this exposure and may not handle it well. The ego may well be misunderstood.

To venture, to risk, to put your neck on the line, is to act like every famous inventor, soldier and adventurer throughout history. The entrepreneur should be admired and respected. So, whether they like it or not, the entrepreneur will display their ego, somehow.

The difference between an entrepreneur compared to a celebrity is that the ego needs to be matched with humility – without this it will cause jealousy. The celebrity usually has exceptional musical, sporting or acting talent. The entrepreneur was one of us ordinary folk. Their ego can be easily misunderstood.

Adventurers and the great masses of those fallen in battle more often than not gave the ultimate sacrifice. The same can be said, in part, for the entrepreneur who may sacrifice their health, family and financial safety. Wins and gains come at a cost, as will be discussed later. But not often the ultimate sacrifice. Suicides do occur when entrepreneurs are unable to face failure. Entrepreneurs are, often, obsessive characters. Their ego is an interesting part of their DNA.

Of the Entrepreneur

The term entrepreneur is a loanword from French and was first defined by the Irish-French economist Richard Cantillon (1680-1734), "as the person who pays a certain price for a product to then resell it at an uncertain price, thereby making decisions about obtaining and using the resources while consequently admitting the risk of enterprise."

The term has been used and modified regularly since, perhaps the latest being 1985 when an entrepreneur was defined as a person who started a new business where there was none before.

There are different types of entrepreneur:

Firstly, the one-man-band who sustains themselves and is self-employed, not salaried, is probably not really an entrepreneur per the above definition, but gets by and earns a living.

Secondly the person who is in business, who employs a couple of other people and makes a living, could be classed as an entrepreneur 'of sorts'. Again not particularly entrepreneurial but they do support themself and others.

Thirdly, we are concentrating our study on the businessperson who develops an organisation, employs a team, invests in plant and creates a business that can be sold as a going concern. That is entrepreneurial and is our first rank of a real entrepreneur.

Lastly, our other entrepreneurs are those who sell their businesses for an amount in excess of a comfortable sum and can retire without financial concerns. Also those really rich and successful entrepreneurs who can not only afford to retire but also to reinvest and encourage and mentor others are in another class and ones to whom we all aspire.

These words of clarification, of course, allow us to relate the empathy and our own egos with our subject matter. Their success and position in society will be discussed many times in the following chapters. As you read on, please do not lose sight of the fact that the entrepreneur often fails, but they have at least tried. Serial failure makes them a fool and not an entrepreneur.

So the entrepreneur is a risk-taker and adventurer, through business. Also, they are a person who the world would miss were they not to exist. Therefore they are a very important person. They enable the rest of us to enjoy our lives with comfort, up-to-date gadgets and food without toil. How we got here today is because of the entrepreneurs from previous generations. We have a lot to be thankful for.

1.3 The rise of the new entrepreneur

As a result of rapidly changing times we need to recognise the new generation of entrepreneurs. A 'new entrepreneur' is emerging who uses new tools with new distribution channels and new markets as part of the new internet age. However the new entrepreneur is actually the same entrepreneur as past generations, with the same basic characteristics, just using today's tools.

So what are the tools to becoming an entrepreneur in today's world? Age, culture, social background and education do not, nor should not, preclude anyone from any social position becoming an entrepreneur.

£££ OUR SURVEY ASKED:

Was a parent an entrepreneur or businessperson?

Yes: 36%

No: 64%

Entrepreneurialism is not a gene.

Capitalism is not a mistake, but part of an evolutionary path. Hundreds of books have appeared in very recent years to explain the financial crisis of the past five years, in the context of the development of the Western world. These books try to explain the rise and development of capitalism, as practised by the entrepreneur, as being a part of an on-going process of evolution, mainly explained as a social evolution. There are various reasons put forward which suggest that the capitalist theory is wrong and leads to hardship. Considering this backdrop, the entrepreneur often can be vilified. Such vilification is much mistaken as at least he is attempting to make good for himself and others.

Capitalism is currently seen as the end-point of social evolution. This is mainly because there has been no alternative put forward, not even as a result of the most recent history and experience being the deepest world-wide recession in living history. A recession can be good. It creates a lack of demand for some products and a demand for the right products at the right price. It stops over-capacity. It allows asset values to adjust to their correct position, to be affordable in real terms and not on borrowed terms.

Those that fail were weak, sad as it is to say. Technology is changing and developing rapidly. New methods, new ways and a new age create new demands. The entrepreneur has to be alive to and aware of those changes. The new entrepreneur in today's world meets those demands in new industries with new technology and processes.

Leading British politicians talk about a 'third way' or a 'big society' however they have an elastic and convenient way of allowing government to condemn market excesses while entrenching market forces in every corner of society. Clarity is required to determine which areas of society should be ruled by the market and which should not. It appears that the language of ethics has been usurped by that of economics.

The entrepreneur needs to stand firm and display the stoicism of yesteryear. At one time it was the army, the church, medicine or even education which could offer progression and opportunity, a stable livelihood and a good reputation. Trade would linger behind.

Since the middle of the 20th century, careers in accounting, law, banking and stockbroking attracted the cream of the graduate population. As a result, there was a high barrier to entry and these careers produced, inevitably, long-term security.

This path was about to come to an abrupt and sudden end. Possibly this occurred at the turn of the century without anyone realising. There was no longer a safe road to retirement or a job for life. The new norm is not of growth and safety but of sluggish economic development and 'job hopping'. Careers are self-made, not handed out by birth right or study.

Wage stagnation will enlighten youth to become new entrepreneurs through sheer zeal.

There have been three major changes to the world-wide economic arena since 2000.

Firstly, when the financial services sector was deregulated in the 1980s, and professional services and financial services proliferated as a result to accommodate the expansion, the top-paying jobs grew in banking and related industries in the city. The best intellectual minds in science, engineering, mathematics and even languages found their fortune on the trading floors not the law courts. Business and trade were to become no match for any other industry. No-one could foresee the international banking crisis of 2007 onwards and its widespread consequences. As fast as bankers' reputation was forged, it was damaged for generations to come. As round after round of redundancy, crisis and scandal occurred, the industry lurched from headline to headline. The fundamentals of a sound economy are a sound banking system and this is now in doubt, worldwide. The reputations and the capital bases of the banks need to recover. This will not be an overnight turnaround.

Secondly, the growth (and domination) of hedge funds, futures and derivatives as being a normal trading practice has confounded many in the financial sector. This book is not to cover nor comment on these products but those in that sector may not now know who any lender, borrower or backer of last resort would be. Most countries by this fact alone are bust. This, in itself, can only create turmoil and further instability on a much more immediate scale if confidence were to erode at some stage in the future.

Thirdly, the emergence and now complete dominance of the internet and communications have transformed how business copes with the instant demands of today's markets. No business can afford to operate offline. Without a website you are not worth looking at, let alone trading with. The speed and ease of modern communication makes any decision, trade or transaction possible within seconds at any time of the day, in any part of the world, with almost any product or service!

With the introduction of the internet and its worldwide and everyday use, there comes a fundamental change in job opportunities, careers and, as a result – the future for the entrepreneur.

So, it is possible therefore to create a business from scratch with a skeleton team, located in various different parts of the country or countries, generating sales or services on a low budget. What is not required now is as important as what was required. This is mainly:

- no premises,

- no teams of people,

- no large stockholding,

- no infrastructure, filing and storage, a limited back office,

- no high street presence,

- no large paper trails nor processes.

Therefore, as a result of these three dramatic changes, a new determination will be required against a backdrop of unstable banking, amidst possible turmoil and definitely new tools are needed.

A new path to success has emerged for today's entrepreneur while the barrier to entry is vastly reduced.

£££ OUR SURVEY ASKED:
At what age did you want your own business?
On average aged 27

At what age did you start your first business?
On average aged 33

At what age did consider yourself to be successful?
On average aged 48

At what age do you wish to sell or retire?
No specific answers given

Our highly successful entrepreneur who mentioned their 'DNA and experience in early years' can be classified as needing those first few years at work to gain experience. From the above it can be foreseen that the average age at which people want to have their own business will reduce significantly in the next generation possibly to 22, being immediately after graduation or college.

The age at which people will start their business will reduce from 33 to perhaps 26.

The key statistic to take from this specific question in our survey is that 15 years of hard work, graft, determination and self-sacrifice was required to be successful at, on average, aged 48. It would be pure conjecture to state that the 15 years will shorten, but the immediacy of wants and demands of today's results-driven world (take Premier League football for example) will probably make that come true too. The successful entrepreneur may look to put in, on average, less than 10 years' work at his business, otherwise he could become bored, may sell or perhaps lose interest and failure will follow. Timescales are shortening.

Given that conjecture then, success will arrive in the late 30s, 10 years ahead of this generation. What will they do with their time after that?

The success of the founders of Google, Facebook, Amazon, Twitter et al inspire the best of the talented young minds.

However, new industries are not limited to internet-driven distribution channels. There are innovative businesses developing in fashion, media, entertainment, arts and clean energy and life sciences. Never before, since perhaps the introduction of the railroads, has so much change happened so quickly. The railroads enabled mass travel. The internet enables mass communication.

So the recession of the last few years is not so much as a recession as a revolution. Reading 'Manias, Panics and Crashes' by Charles Kindleberger and Robert Aliber reveals that crisis is not so much a life-changing event as a way of life. Their appendix lists 40 such events in history from 1618 to 2008. This reflects a recession, panic, mania, crash or scandal hitting the worldwide markets every 10 years throughout the industrialised period of western history.

How do our entrepreneurs cope with that turmoil? Or is it really turmoil and is it the norm?

Government has a clear role to play in encouraging the entrepreneur. In the UK there have been many schemes to attract investment for business and provide tax relief for the investor.

Government also has an even clearer role in ensuring that the entrepreneur himself is encouraged and not dis-incentivised due to taxation, regulation or red tape. However, governments seem to be very shy at siding with that social class, as it seems an unpopular catchphrase with the masses, but how else will there be innovation or even job creation? (See Chapter 9.2)

Is it too soon to predict that this century will be a repeat of say 200 to 250 years ago when the industrial revolution first began? Will it be the age of the entrepreneur, with new tools and new industries and low barriers to entry? Almost certainly – in which case we need to fully understand the entrepreneur. Financiers, banks and backers need to sympathise with their profile.

There are a number of questions here, and they can be answered.

Napoleon called the English a nation of shopkeepers, first mentioned in 1776 by Adam Smith in his epistle a 'wealth of nations'. While this book is aimed at a worldwide audience, this obvious sea change in doing business and the revolution of the past 30 years is best demonstrated by recent findings.

Research shows that closures in the high street in the UK for example, have been mainly computer game shops, health food outlets and card shops, only to be replaced by payday loan shops, pawnbrokers, pound shops, charity outlets and betting shops, intermingled with coffee houses. Retail on the high street is a big issue for the future. Demand and the internet have clearly replaced the need for the former and the latter are perhaps becoming meeting places, settings for a new social scene facilitated via the social networking of the internet. Licensed premises are closing weekly.

Political parties in the UK, particularly the Conservatives and social democrats accepted in the 1980s that there was a central role for markets in the economy and also believed that the National Health Service, along with most public services, should operate outside of the market. Today, market concepts are applied in every sphere of human activity and such a stance 30 years ago is almost unthinkable. Opportunities for the entrepreneur are there to be taken. Short termism abounds as a result. As mentioned above, the barriers to entry are lowered and the industry sectors widened. Is the 'luck' mentioned by 96% of those surveyed actually the ability of our new entrepreneurs to see opportunities and to take them – in the world of today.

Capitalism may be one, if not the only, game in town, but it may not be compatible with every aspect of life. To accept capitalism fully and to attempt to make it compatible with the majority of life, the entrepreneur who creates that culture must be understood and incentivised.

There must be empathy with the ego of the entrepreneur.

Entrepreneurialism is good not bad.

1.4 The contents

This book contains seven sections, with the eighth being the conclusion.

Of course, most people drive and most families possess a car. Also there are many models from which to choose. Once successful, the entrepreneur often likes an expensive car of their choice to enhance their image and status and it is, as the scriptwriter would say, 'to demonstrate clearly the proof of scene'.

The car chosen is normally a certain brand or size and exudes the apparent success, but hey, he deserves it. Already we are judging our entrepreneur prematurely... before we have even read a section of this book. Do they really deserve this manifest and brazen token of opulence?

This book is sectioned with sub-titles relating to the motor vehicle – mainly as a bit of fun and to make the read interesting.

The basic model

This section examines intelligence, luck, whether there is a right time or right place and whether the entrepreneur goes out of their way to establish a successful business or whether it actually finds them. It is important to note that each of these have a great part to play in the entrepreneur's success. But are these aspects so critical?

Factory-fitted extras

This section describes the make-up of an entrepreneur and deals with his psychology, the range of character types on offer and which best suits him. How we would recognise the entrepreneur, together with the good and bad bits of his character. Also, how they, and those around them, can deal with their ego. It is imperative at this juncture to appreciate their approach to acute issues such as attitude to risk and materialism, payback and financial rewards. Do they deserve the car?

The test drive

This gives us signs of their approach to management and how they relate to others. Considerations include whether the entrepreneur can deal with their growing business and how they put their own 'stamp' on the business without allowing it to spoil or dilute the business. The car is well on its journey by now! Can the entrepreneur keep it on the road?

Going up the gears

We now are in the arena of success – what happens next? How does the entrepreneur relate to issues and how should those around react to them? How does the entrepreneur develop their close team and members of the board or inner circle? Do they understand their customers and their need for service? Can they be side-tracked into developing that new product or do they stay with what they know best? Do they stay with their core product or service? How dangerous is it to diversify? The need for an overall strategy surely delivers success.

The Sunday drive

There are many social issues facing an entrepreneur in today's society. These are discussed with particular reference to the social scene, personal life and health, as well as the public reaction to high profile entrepreneurs, as the media portray them. Also, in life many ordinary people face addictions. Whether this is with drugs, alcohol, smoking, gambling or sex – the entrepreneur faces the same vices, and with funds available the vices are perhaps more easily accessible. All of these are covered in this chapter together with the important issue often experienced by the entrepreneur and those closely around him: how do they deal with the pathological character weakness of opulence and spending?

The 'trade in'

A successful entrepreneur will, over time, wish to realise their 'favourite' asset: to be able to look back and possibly retire with sufficient money in the bank. Are they a 'one- trick-pony or do they serially invest? And if so, with success or not?

Who can use this manual?

It's important to know that this book, manual or 'teach in' is of use to many. Parts of it can be used for better awareness for all those who deal with the entrepreneur and of course there are many budding entrepreneurs - do you have what it takes? This book should clarify the ingredients required. Should you back the entrepreneur who presents their business case so well - do they have what it takes?

Conclusion

An important part of any work. This is the summary which puts it all into context to make you stop and think again.

Just before we start the car and drive it out of the garage on to the road – some thoughts.

There is no other word for entrepreneur, but to save typing each time we could use businessperson, risk-taker, odd ball .....but entrepreneur will do.

We have not spoken yet about money or potential riches. Let's leave that until the appropriate time. Motivation is discussed throughout and, as you will already realise, money is most often the motivating force.

The above should excite and motivate you to read further. This will be an interesting ride. It will not be rocky or dangerous but may take you down some turnings you had not even thought were there.

The entrepreneur is probably society's most interesting 'type' as they can come from any walk of life and do not necessarily have a natural singing, acting, sporting and political talent. The sports stars, film celebrities and famous singers including all the 'A'-listers can be catapulted to fame and adulation overnight and, as a direct result, may need psychiatric and clinical help for addiction as they don't operate in the same controlled lifestyle as the average person.

Neither does the entrepreneur, but they strive to get 'there' to be successful. It may take time, unlike the stars mentioned in the preceding paragraph, and often they do not realise where 'there' is. Being close to them is very difficult, too. Most often they need the average person alongside helping them and that is where **we** fit in.

So now let's meet our entrepreneurs, put on your belts and strap up…

CHAPTER TWO

THE BASIC MODEL

2.1 Introduction

One of the best ways to empathise with an entrepreneur is to analyse their inner psyche, character and personality.

This section will analyse the intelligence, luck, place and timing of the 'would be' entrepreneur to see if there is any common thread to achieving success.

Are they more intelligent?

Is it as simple as throwing a dice, as mentioned in the introduction? If so, then, just as the dice will be equally likely to come up with 'one' to 'six' in six throws, why is every other venture not successful or at least why is success not compatible with the known averages? If it is that easy to become an entrepreneur, then why doesn't everyone try it? Why do so many say that the successful entrepreneurs have been lucky? It is not that simple. This section explains what is needed.

And is it just down to the sector and ensuring that you are the market leader or first to market in that sector? Surely not? Sector helps, but is not the end game.

A great car has a smooth-running engine. This is what will make the entrepreneur work to maximum performance.

2.2 Is it intelligence?

The normal progress for everyone aged 5 to 16 is to receive full-time education and be subject to regular external tests.

The aim of these tests is to measure what is considered to be intelligence, as we know it. A satisfactory pass mark in these external tests may often be as low as 51%. The actual result may be even higher. An 'A' grade may be achieved at a mark of say 70% and above. While passing an exam is good, and shows moderate intelligence, achieving an 'A' grade is considered objectively as showing intelligence.

The questions to be raised with this system are:

- Do the tests at that moderately low level of success give us a fair indication of intelligence?

- Do the tests concentrate on the full variety of attributes and skills required for later life?

- Could it be considered that these tests are "one dimensional" and clearly do not take into account a vast number of factors of intelligence. Those who have failed these tests are almost certainly thrown to the waste heap before life starts – at 16. Yet a few of those 'scrapped' become successful, if not very successful.

Also, intelligence is measured by the grade or grades achieved but the difference between a grade A, B or C may be only be a few marks yet can mean the external verification for that student to allow them to move on to further education or not, as the person so wishes.

An awful lot can depend on these scores and this scoring system, which is so rigidly applied. There are various stages in early life where one can be excluded from moving forward and achieving even moderate success as a direct reason of this process and system. Do you recognise this?

So this current system and marking is not just a question of passing or failing but also (allegedly) a clear measurement of intelligence, as we know it. Someone with an 'A' grade can be considered more intelligent than a person with a 'B'. This could be the difference of one mark or even half a mark but chalks you up or down for life (or until the next retake). It is accepted that there has to be a dividing line somewhere. However the lack of dimension can easily steer many students away from studies and exams.

£££ OUR SURVEY ASKED:
What level of education do you have?
The answers were:

No external examinations	12%
O level or GCSE	68%
A level	56%
HND or other	16%
Degree	40%
Masters	12%
Professional qualification	48%
Other	24%

It is clear from these results that a formal education as we know it is not essential to a successful entrepreneurial career. Only 40% interviewed had degrees, albeit that is higher than the national average, but 12% had no external examination at all. Are they stupid? Certainly not. They had, and have, other skills.

£££ OUR SURVEY ASKED:
Do you think that a formal education to degree level is important for entrepreneurs?
92% answered no, with only 8% answering yes.

Success with this current way of measuring intelligence is found in many entrepreneurs as they have had successful academic careers, but it is not the be all and end all. Many entrepreneurs do not relish detailed study simply because they possess other skills, and other forms of intelligence. It is wrong to exclude those who have not had success with education as being 'written off' and unable to be successful business people.

Those who are successful at these examinations then have the opportunity to move on to other further, more difficult, tests, which are generally considered to be, and reflect, higher intelligence. Therefore the youngster moves from tests at an early age of 11 for selection and streaming into other external tests at 16 and 18 where they are measured against an assumed average or universally accepted pass mark to establish how they are suited for further education, life in general and of course, future job prospects.

At 18, school leavers enter higher education such as college or university. Achieving a degree can lead to further revered and admired qualifications, such as a masters and a doctorate.

£££ OUR SURVEY ASKED:
Do you think that while a formal education may not be important, that some selling experience in the work environment, at least, is important?
The answer was more or less the same as above with 91% agreeing.

So our successful entrepreneurs would consider that lifetime experiences, not formal education, and a sales environment are more important to becoming an entrepreneur.

There are also other measures of intelligence such as IQ tests and membership of Mensa. These take the form of logical and mathematical questions fired quickly. In this test a mark of 90 or below means sub-normality and 160 and above, brilliance. Every application or test continues to be very one-dimensional. Life repeats itself as the same applies, taking a test and being categorised as a result of its marking and outcome until you become a successful entrepreneur and that outcome can be a surprise to some.

Where do our entrepreneurs sit with this grading, marking and normal acceptance of intelligence? There is no 'normal', there is nothing that says that an 'A' grader will be good in business. There is no direct correlation.

So let us consider how many entrepreneurs that you know or have met have a masters degree, first-class degree, or if no degree, then a string of 'A' grades and a successful academic career behind them? Probably, the answer is very few. In practice, very few entrepreneurs possess master's degrees. Those that do are probably inventors.

Our survey revealed 12% had a 'Masters' qualification.

The standard form of intelligence, which is taught in schools, which means that you learn from text books and reiterate that learning in either coursework or exams is considered very one dimensional when you consider the work and analysis required by an entrepreneur. The entrepreneur has to balance so many balls and plates in the air at any one time as he goes about his business, that there could not possibly be any examination on entrepreneurship? That would be the last subject that could be taught didactically.

So the hypothesis is what sort of intelligence do these entrepreneurs have, who clearly are, and come across as being, intelligent but not, under acceptable 'normal' intelligence standards as taught, marked and graded.

For that type of understanding we need to look in detail at alternative measures of intelligence. This is simple, as the work has been done for us, but what is not simple is putting our classic entrepreneur into one of the pigeon holes from the analysis undertaken.

The measurement we are going to apply is Howard Gardner's theory of multiple intelligences. This is essential to evaluate the intelligence of our entrepreneur. A doctorate does not exist in the world of the entrepreneur. The equivalent of doctorate is perhaps how much money they have made. Once we have analysed where our entrepreneur shows his intelligence they will be easier to understand and empathy can occur.

The multiple measures of intelligences (seven in total) by Howard Gardner was published in 1983. As a result of there being little empirical evidence to support his theory it has not progressed as much as a form of work as many think it should. It is subjective, but once we match and map our entrepreneur to the theory, you will see it come alive. Gardner later added four more types of intelligence making eleven in total.

The psychology of the entrepreneur will not fit with all of them.

To quote a review of his work in 1993, Gardner said:

> "In the heyday of psychometric and behaviourist eras, it was generally believed that intelligence was a single entity that was inherited; and that human beings – initially a blank slate – could be trained to learn anything, provided that it was presented in an appropriate way. Nowadays an increasing number of researchers believe precisely the opposite; that there exists a multitude of intelligence, quite independent of each other, that each intelligence has its own strengths and constraints; that the mind is far from unencumbered at birth; and that it is unexpectedly difficult to teach things that go against early naïve theories that challenge the natural lines of force within an intelligence and its matching domains."

It is considered that there are various forms of intelligence. The seven levels are:

Logical / Mathematical intelligence

This is the capacity to analyse problems logically, carry out mathematical calculations and investigate issues scientifically. In Gardner's terms, it entails the ability to detect patterns, reason deductively and think logically. Our entrepreneur needs to know at a glance, intuitively or even instinctively when the numbers add up to make a profit.

Interpersonal intelligence

This is the capacity to understand the intentions, motivations and desires of other people. It allows people to work effectively with others. Educators, sales people, religious and political leaders and counsellors all need a well-developed if not first-class proficiency in interpersonal intelligence. Communication is key. Our entrepreneur needs to show a talent in encouraging, leading, giving examples and selling to others.

Intrapersonal intelligence

This entails the capacity to understand oneself, to appreciate one's feelings, fears and motivations. In Gardner's view it involves having an effective working model of ourselves and to be able to use such information to regulate our lives

Linguistic intelligence

This involves sensitivity to spoken and written language and the ability to learn languages and the capacity to use language to accomplish certain goals. This intelligence includes the ability to effectively use language to express oneself rhetorically or poetically; and language as a means to remember information. Writers, poets, lawyers and speakers are among those that Gardner cites in this category, but obviously it covers all those who are highly skilled and deal with the written word. This is not important for our entrepreneur, but helpful.

Spatial intelligence

This involves the potential to recognise and use the patterns of wide and more confined space. Perhaps Gardner was thinking along the lines of those who operate vehicles or machinery and even architects, in this area of intelligence. Given that at the moment there is no other category, the view commonly held would be that a form of spatial intelligence provides vision. Perhaps vision is an overriding skill of the entrepreneur or are they just trying their luck. Certainly the serial entrepreneur is just trying to find something to stick at, which is successful, but those who know that a product, service or solution will work, do have vision. This will be covered more in the section on 'luck'.

Bodily-kinaesthetic intelligence

This entails the potential of using one's whole body or parts of the body to solve problems. It is the ability to use mental abilities to coordinate bodily movements. Gardner sees mental and physical activity as related and of course, top class sportsmen have this intelligence. Again our entrepreneur may use this skill, in part, if they have carried out manual work ahead of their success as an entrepreneur and again may use this skill, as with music, for relaxation purposes, too.

Musical intelligence

This involves skill in the performance, composition and appreciation of musical patterns. According to Gardner this form runs in an almost structural parallel to linguistic intelligence. Any entrepreneur possessing this intelligence would almost certainly operate within this industry, perhaps as a performer but generally may use this for relaxation, if it is possessed in any degree of competence.

£££ OUR SURVEY ASKED:

Rank these forms of intelligence out of 7 and also to score their importance out of 10.

The answers were:	Average Rank	Average Score of Importance
Interpersonal	6.12	7.84
Logical and mathematical	5.96	8.60
Intrapersonal	5.36	7.04
Linguistic	3.64	4.24
Spatial	3.32	3.32
Bodily kinaesthetic	2.48	3.20
Musical	1.12	1.92

So, in summary, it is generally considered that the entrepreneur must be very mathematical and logical, and have excellent interpersonal communication skills. No entrepreneur can survive without these key aptitudes to a very high level. They are the two clear winners with a close third being the intra personal skill which involves a clear understanding of one's own feelings. Please read those meanings above once more for these three attributes. Do you have these?

The selling experience referred to earlier and the ability to relate to others scores high and comes through strongly with the survey, first in fact. Does this mean that interpersonal pastimes such as sport during school and one's youth allow the entrepreneur to develop this skill – almost certainly.

Sport provides the thrill of winning both in terms of team or individual success, by scoring hundreds, hitting hat-tricks and achieving record times. This is set alongside the humility required in defeat and being bowled for a 'duck', missing short putts, letting in soft goals or simply losing by the narrowest of margins. Sport develops character.

Logical and mathematical intelligence is ranked 2nd, but scored higher in terms of average importance. It is therefore very important to understand mathematics, such as the break-even position of your business, the figures, the footfall, an average spend per customer, and perhaps the profits achieved and even the warehouse capacity. A logical brain is also key, to be able to ascertain a critical path to get things done in a practical order and to follow a process. A formal mathematical training in the profit and loss statement or a balance sheet, is not so important – we shall get to that.

The entrepreneur needs to show tremendous drive and enthusiasm, often against common and well-held opinion. Therefore the intrapersonal skill of being able to have a clear strength of character but also self-discipline is essential.

In respect of communication and interpersonal skills above, it is only verbal and written skills are considered. Written skills are only considered at an average level and not, in the first instance, as a highly talented key skill to the level of learning languages and literary accomplishment. So, linguistic intelligence is not required at a high skill level to be an entrepreneur. It ranks 4th.

Vision, clearly relative to spatial intelligence, is required.

Bodily-kinaesthetic intelligence can be considered useful but not 'front line'. As described above, musical intelligence would only be required if the entrepreneur operated in that industry.

Therefore, three intelligences are key. Two are not essential but useful and perhaps two not at all. The entrepreneur is definitely proving to be a rounded individual.

Gardner argued, as we do here, that:

> "people have a unique blend of intelligences. He argued that the big challenge facing the deployment of human resources 'is how to best take advantage of the uniqueness conferred on us as a species exhibiting several intelligences'."

The entrepreneur ignores others and ploughs on regardless, operating with their own intelligence, hope and vision. Good for them.

It would be wrong to consider these seven intelligences without including the four additional ones. We need to respect Gardner's work – it is ground-breaking, and while the education system continues with one-dimensional measurement as a form of safety, as it is argued 'why break what is not broken', it does not allow academic 'failures' to feel successful. Such people need an overdose of intrapersonal intelligence and drive to succeed – the 'will to win' or 'hunger'. The drive so often mentioned in our survey.

However, four additional intelligences, as described by Gardner, rarely apply to the entrepreneur. These are:

Naturalistic intelligence

This enables human beings to recognise, categorise and draw upon certain features of the environment.

Spiritual intelligence

This relates to claims surrounding truth and the need for it to be partially identified by others. This intelligence obviously encompasses spiritual or religious aspects.

Existential intelligence

This relates to a concern with 'ultimate' issues. Perhaps this does relate back to the vision that we feel our entrepreneur possesses. Gardner's theory does start to clutch at straws at this stage. The inclusion of both spiritual and existential intelligences without clear definition probably over-extends the wonderful theory portrayed by Gardner in his earlier work and so clearly demonstrated here.

Moral intelligence is Gardner's final category and he suggests this about a concern for rules and behaviours that govern the sanctity of life. If we accept a moral realm it is then possible to speak of moral intelligence. It is argued that morality is about the kind of person rather than an intelligence. Unless we stop there, or Gardner stops there, this list could be boundless. Integrity is often referred to in the survey in skills under the free format answer, which we shall investigate in Chapter 3 under character types. Please note its inclusion here as a form of intelligence. Integrity and as a result responsibility is an essential character attribute of the successful entrepreneur.

Having discussed intelligence and the one-dimensional measurements used in the academic world and applied that in other dimensions, it is clear the entrepreneur is intelligent.

It is fair to say that there are some clear areas of intelligence possessed by any entrepreneur and we should include those as we see them occur on a regular basis.

The entrepreneur is:

- logical and mathematical,

- good with people,

- knows himself - in terms of strengths and weaknesses.

Possesses clear skills in being:

- sharp and quick witted,

- and clearly visionary.

Overall, they are driven and perhaps obsessively, so.

There is no measure using empirical evidence (such as in the academic world) that would allow the entrepreneur to score 51% in a test on any of these subjects. As mentioned above, the entrepreneur's success is that others wish to do business with him and of course, people will work for him. They find him engaging, dynamic and other adjectives more suited to the discussion on character type. A psychological profiling would demonstrate these attributes.

The discussion above proves that successful entrepreneurs are intelligent, in a way, in their own way. They may be sharp and quick-witted but not possess a formal education, as such. They also gain skills and knowledge during their career, being a form of intelligence and mature with that knowledge.

Some entrepreneurs may rue their lack of attention in the classroom in their youth. As their career progresses they discover and re-learn certain basic skills which are required. They can 'upskill' in those, such as accounting, languages or report writing

2.3 Or luck?

Many say that the successful entrepreneur is lucky. 96% did so in our survey.

Luck is defined as being 'the recipient of good fortune which is beyond one's control'.

More often than not this is tinged with a touch of jealousy. The statement sounds like a slur against the entrepreneur. The person making the statement clearly has neither success nor wealth and cannot work out or establish why the entrepreneur does. They forget the intelligence, skill or just damn hard work and prefer to call it 'luck'.

So what is luck? Can it be measured? Is success a likely or a probable outcome?

The study of statistics has established the theory of probability. Probability theory concerns the concept that an event will occur and the likely chance of success or outcome. The incidence that a statement is true, could be another example.

In respect of our entrepreneurs, the likelihood of success is not down to luck. They cannot throw a dice and bank on the result being heads or tails. There are no 'either/or' results. The events are not mutually exclusive but there is a degree of likely outcomes. The entrepreneur can fail or be extremely successful. Generally we only hear of those who are successful. The failure is like the poor academic consigned to the scrap heap until he tries again, learns by his mistakes and thereby eventually, hopefully succeeds.

£££ OUR SURVEY ASKED:
Do you feel that, in general, a previous business failure helps an entrepreneur succeed?
76% answered yes

If becoming an entrepreneur and being successful was all about being lucky then with enough throws of the dice, in time, everyone would be an entrepreneur and successful at it. It is only a question of exhausting all possibilities. But endless energy, finance and time is not in your favour.

The University of Tennessee analysed business failures from start-ups and found that there were several clear, major causes of failure. A start-up is defined as a business that fails within the first three years. The report was verified in 2012.

46% of businesses fail due to incompetence.

Therefore senior management, if not our entrepreneur, needs to be competent, not only in his skill or product but in his management. The reasons given were:

- emotionally over or under-pricing, ie setting the prices too high or too low (at the outset) for the market for the product or service on offer through misconception.

- living expenses too high for the business, ie drawing too much from the business starving it of a vital resource such as cash.

- non-payment of taxes, ie creating a back log of liabilities that suddenly catches up with the business and spikes cash flow, is perhaps unexpected and is unaffordable in the ordinary auspices of working capital. This area also, perhaps, displays a lack of compliance in a sophisticated society or organisational skills.

- no knowledge of pricing, ie as above, pricing product or service incorrectly, creating no sales at all, if overpriced or unsustainable losses on market share if underpriced see Laker Airways v BA (1982)).

- lack of planning, ie a lack of strategic plan and direction, which can be fatal if the wrong move is made.

- no knowledge of financing, ie, a lack of knowledge of the creation of profit, the need for investment and its affordability and the sources of finance for the business and working capital.

- no experience of record-keeping, ie poor house-keeping. It is so important to track the businesses success, its weaknesses and potential for improvement.

All of these reasons are based on financial decisions rather than the lack of sales, say, or poor marketing. It is almost a given fact that with more competent financial management and/ or more financial resources and time that an entrepreneur would succeed in running a business. We have not considered market rejection or reduced sales, and instead have focused entirely on the 'internal competence' of the entrepreneur.

Poor economic conditions, such as a recession, do not have a negative impact on an entrepreneur's success, unless they have limited knowledge of finance. This will be discussed later under the theories on the start-up. Reference will be made to the above list through the following chapters. A recession does change the marketplace's way of thinking and businesses need to be adequately resourced to counter this. There are clearly some business types which suffer greatly in recession, such as retail, property development and anything associated with a discretionary spend. However, these factors seem to be eliminated from the causes above which entirely reflect on the skill set and attitude of the entrepreneur to running his venture.

30% then fail due to unbalanced expertise or a lack of experience.

The reasons given were:

- poor credit-granting practices, ie making the sale but not collecting the cash. This is fatal.

- too-rapid expansion, ie this is commonly known by bankers as overtrading and by entrepreneurs as success, but leads back to adequate resourcing, principally cash. Of course, businesses can run out of stock or human resources to service customers, too. This can quickly lead to customer dissatisfaction.

- inadequate borrowing practice. Not recognising the need for working capital (and some for that lean period which every business experiences).

Again, these causes are extremely financially biased.

The third and last major category, at **11%, cited a lack of experience in line of goods or services.**

The details for this category were:

- carrying inadequate inventory stock or skills base, ie as above under 'too rapid expansion', however this could also include under-resourcing and not identifying key products quickly enough.

- lack of knowledge of suppliers or resources, ie buying inadequately in terms of price or quality, and competitors taking advantage.

- wasting advertising and marketing budget, ie common for entrepreneurs with an ego. It is so easy to write a cheque and advertise in the wrong areas, entertain the wrong people and hire expensive marketing consultants to promote products in the wrong areas.

This is more like it. The above three are all decisions that the visionary (and clever) entrepreneur will investigate and use to create his own bank of knowledge.

So with 76% of failures being based on a lack of financial prowess and expertise, then 24% of failures are based on the market or the business being insufficiently resourced.

The leading management mistakes were:

- going into business for the wrong reasons, ie having nowhere else to go, having been laid-off or released from an existing employer and thinking that it is easy to start up. Inadequate investigation of the market and subject matter.

- taking advice from family and friends, ie not seeking professional advice and taking a step back as to what is actually trying to be achieved.

- being in the wrong place at the wrong time, ie not understanding that certain sectors are dying, that a recession is looming or a major business is closing, which will have a dramatic effect on a local area.

- underestimating the time and energy required, ie not giving the business enough time and underestimating the level of commitment needed.

- family pressures on time and money,

- pride ie, the ego gets in the way and poor decisions are made such as spending lavishly and unnecessarily.

- lack of market awareness, ie a lack of understanding of the actual product and service on offer from competitors and failure to adjust accordingly.

- the entrepreneur falls in love with the product or business, ie makes 'non-business based decisions' such as opening up in a town with too many competitors based on pride and because they think they will succeed. 'Success is a lousy teacher. It seduces you into thinking you cannot lose'. See below under 3.4 'Taking risks'.

- lack of financial responsibility and awareness, as discussed above.

- lack of a clear focus, see below under 'Strategic planning'.

- too much money. This often not cited, however working with 'daddy's money' can result in a lack of responsibility and the hunger and desire required to succeed. It is often said that 'immigrants' desire and borrowing leads to greater success in business.

These findings reveal that the entrepreneurs clearly did not realise their own shortcomings, nor the ingredients required to make their business succeed. They themselves would no doubt put it down to sheer bad luck. Their core competencies are lacking, clearly. That cannot be put down to luck.

UK reports show that at least 500,000 people start a new business each year and 51% fail in the first year. The reasons cited for starting a business are being one's own boss, freedom, work-life balance and being in control. As a result of the long hours for very little reward and not being able to afford to hire staff at the outset the work-life balance can slip out of balance and control. They then can become highly reactive with no goals, no strategic vision or direction and no time to plan or think. Failure rates are accordingly high and get higher, as discussed above, in the first 3 years.

None of that is caused by bad luck. Being successful is therefore not lucky.

OUR SURVEY ASKED...

...the entrepreneurs to rank what they thought the main reason is that businesses fail, from the following 6*:

	Average rank out of 6
Insufficient capital and finance	4.36
Recession and outside forces	3.88
Lack of strategic direction	3.68
Owner's excessive drawings	3.36
Insufficient financial information	3.08
Failure to pay government taxes	2.76

*(the free format response is mentioned in chapter 3.4)

Some successful businesses receive lucky breaks throughout their duration. These favourable turns obviously have a much more dramatic effect at the beginning or in the early years of trading.

Lucky breaks (remember luck is defined as being the recipient of good fortune which is beyond one's control) can take the form of:

- winning a relatively large, profitable and sustainable contract,

- a competitor failing with a beneficial knock-on effect,

- a key account supporting a venture,

- favourable financial support,

- generous lease terms.

Then, the entrepreneur should seize the day or rather...seize the opportunity.

Unexpected outturns to plan that are beneficial can be considered luck or lucky. However, clearly seeing an opportunity and having the resource in terms of time and money to take that opportunity and then to have the drive to make it happen and to happen successfully could be analysed as being lucky.

If the entrepreneur has a clear strategic plan, these unexpected outturns can be measured and considered lucky as being clearly favourable events to a well-defined plan. The entrepreneur could be considered to be an opportunist and by taking these opportunities and making them successful, the entrepreneur is by default lucky. Not so, the lucky entrepreneur makes his luck.

Success is the result of what sociologists like to term "accumulative advantage". The entrepreneur can easily not see nor take up all these grants or opportunities. Even if they do take them up, they can still mess them up. The lucky break is not definitive.

Businesses with the best rates of success were highlighted by the University of Tennessee, as well as other sources, and these will be discussed below under 2.5 Sector.

Luck can be defined as the taking of an opportunity when it is presented to you.

Therefore seeing an opportunity, having the ability to take it, act on it and ensure that the end game is successful – is luck. Every entrepreneur will be able to look back on his glittering career and highlight one or more of these 'breaks' and consider it to be fortunate.

2.4 Or just the right time and the right place?

So once we agree that the successful entrepreneur is not just lucky, we can turn our attention to the next piece of vitriol that is hurled his way.

They are 'in the right place at the right time'.

Again, as described above, this can be true to a degree as, of course, a lucky break can come their way but often they earn that rather than it being pure fluke.

Malcolm Gladwell, in his new book 'Outliers', explains some theories concerning this concept. He states that successful people throughout history have been in the right place at the right time.

He analyses skill sets which are developed through practice, such as the 10,000 hours spent practising and honing skills during teenage years in the sports and arts. Yet, looking in detail at a list compiled of the 75 wealthiest people in history, including royalty and contemporary billionaires, such as financial gurus, 14 are born within 9 years of each other in America, between 1831 and 1840.

They came of age in the 1860s and 1870s. The railroads were being built and Wall Street emerged. This was when manufacturing built a new economy and a burgeoning population created a marketplace no one had foreseen.

They were born at the right time. Any earlier or any later and they would have missed it. During this time the US population grew from:

12.8 million in 1830 to

31.4 million in 1860 to

76.1 million 1900.

Accordingly, it is hardly surprising that some entrepreneurs made their fortunes. They were (born) in the right place, at the right time.

However, we are not necessarily trying to analyse or understand the seriously successful or seriously wealthy, just those who happen to make things happen. This is the standard entrepreneur, who perhaps makes a success of his life by creating a business and employing others. There are a tremendous number of these.

They still have to take advantage of opportunities given, but it proves at this 'super' level and of course, at any other, that the right place and the right time helps.

This was repeated later when Silicon Valley in California established the personal computer revolution in 1975. Work backwards to the mid 1950's and review the birth dates of the leaders of that industry and you will see that the seriously successful and wealthy computer moguls were born then, within only three years of each other.

Paul Allen, January 1953

Scott McNealy, November 1954

Vinod Khosla, January 1955

Steve Jobs, February 1955

Eric Schmidt, April 1955

Andy Bechtolsheim, September 1955

Bill Gates, October 1955

Steve Ballmer, March 1956

The analysis proves that they were young enough to play and develop without fearing these new computers. They could risk their early years on such adventures without worrying about the rent, mortgage or feeding their family.

Risk is something we shall come to later but it is evident that this group were in their 20s when Silicon Valley created itself.

As the computer revolution occurred so quickly in such a small area it is hardly surprising that the ages of these computer moguls are so close. The right place and right time occurred here, certainly, but we are investigating the entrepreneur in general, not just a selected few.

The argument is that someone had to be successful, and it was this lot.

If it had not been them, it would have been Harry Smith, Bill Jones or Hank Driberg III, three fictional characters for illustration purposes. The marketplace and industry took the country and world by storm and someone had to be there. So luck does form part of mega success, and so does being in the right place at the right time, but certainly not without:

- earnest endeavour,

- hard work

- and drive as indicated at the outset.

It all goes together.

> **£££ OUR SURVEY ASKED...**
>
> **Do you think you have been in the right place at the right time?**
>
> 84% said yes
>
> **If so please mark its importance to where you are now, out of 10.**
>
> This scored a mark of 7.48

This is an extraordinary result, when you think about it. It means that nearly every successful entrepreneur thinks that their timing has been right.

We shall soon, in turn, be analysing the internet giants of the future or the manufacturers of the next level of robotic beings. How long before the next generation of wealthy yet technical and revolutionary computer entrepreneurs rise to the fore?

The Sunday Times newspaper annually produces a rich list of the wealthiest people. Statistics which review and support the argument above relate to the sixty wealthiest young people (under 30 years old) and where their wealth comes from.

Thirty-three are involved with the media, arts and particularly the music industry. This reinforces the success of the 'X-factor' concept. This is overnight celebrity status which is achieved by winning, or reaching the final stages of a talent show or even exposure on such a show and making a good fist of your performances. Stardom and riches definitely await those noticed. They were in the right place and when we consider their 'sustainability', it will be interesting to see how they progress. It should be the entrepreneurs and businesspeople, not necessarily the stars, that succeed.

Nine are related to technology or internet as you would expect, if not more. The new social media craze is creating further sensational growth on the web, and for those who have got it right, serious wealth at an early age. Blogging and social media have created a massive retail market. Richard Jones for example created Audioscribbler – a database that tracks people's musical tastes – a very clever concept that brings two great industries together. He deserves every success but, of course, history will prove its sustainability.

Eight are in business and retail. These are particularly discount stores, for Robin Arora and Chris Edwards, to distribution, and then recruitment for Louie Evans and Laurence Romeo. Gavin Miller is in the business of care homes for the disadvantaged.

Four have inherited their wealth such as Princes William and Harry. Three are lottery winners and three are in property. The three in property have lived through the past five years of mostly low growth in value, which has led to low levels of wealth in this sector. Considering the property market's record in the last five years compared to the last fifty years there would surely have been more young wealthy entrants included both in terms of numbers in the top 60 by attracting those to this industry and but also wealth in other eras. Not the right time, perhaps.

It can be argued, even for those starting out, that 'right place right time' is important. But it is what they make of it afterwards, how they progress and drive their business forward making decisions bigger than they have before that will prove lasting success.

There are many entrepreneurs who start out with little money and knowledge and grow as they find a niche. That too is about the right time and right place. Jack Cohen who founded Tesco thought that his first pitch would not be his last and his own hard work won the day. Here is a wonderful extract about his early days in business:

> "Upon demobilisation in 1919 he established himself as a market stall holder in Hackney, in London's East End by purchasing surplus NAAFI stock with his demob money. He soon became the owner of a number of market stalls and started a wholesale business. Initially the other stalls were run by members of his family but gradually non-family members were added. Cohen and his wife worked seven days a week, starting at dawn and counting money until late. At each market the traders would

gather and, at a signal, they would race to their favoured pitch. Cohen
could not run fast so he simply threw his cap at the spot and this could
beat anyone. In 1924 he created the Tesco brand..."

So much is encapsulated in this short outline in this section, which will
also be covered later. Many of the mistakes listed above are answered
in this excerpt. Intelligence, luck or being in the 'right place' need to
go in hand with close support from family and just plain endeavour
and hard work.

It cannot be underestimated how much being in the right place and
the right time, such as London after the war with the growing need
for food chains at a mass level assisted Jack Cohen. Also note that by
1900 the meat-packing houses of Chicago had adopted ammonia
cycle commercial refrigeration. In the First World War refrigeration
was used in ammunition factories, therefore its commercial use spread
wide immediately after the Great War, just when Jack Cohen needed it
most to supply and store his goods.

By being in the right place and the right time and along with the right
'extra ingredients' and outside factors, is this luck? Mr Cohen had to
take this opportunity and deal with it accordingly. He demonstrated
intelligence as well as a sharp wit, energy and vision.

2.5 Or the sector?

Not only are carps made about 'the luck' and 'right time and right
place', but it is often said that 'anyone could have sold that product'.
Oh really, if so then why didn't you?

The Sunday Times Rich List for 2012, which analyses more or less
1,000 of the wealthiest people, is made up of 726 self-made millionaires
and 238 who have inherited their wealth.

From totally separate research set out below is an analysis of industries
still operating after four years from start-up. The following are
percentages within each of their own sector:

Finance, insurance and real estate	58%
Education and health	56%
Agriculture	56%
Services	55%

Falling to:

Retail	47%
Transportation, communication and utilities	45%
Information, (obviously risky, whatever your skill levels)	37%

To review those businesses with the worse rate of success after five years they are, in order:

1 Plumbing, heating and air conditioning
2 Single-family house construction (not multiple occupancy such as flats)
3 Grocery stores
4 Restaurants and food outlets
5 Security brokers and dealers
6 Local trucking and transportation

So industry sector can play a part in the success of our entrepreneur. We need to take away from this factors related to timing, such as recessions. No property developer is going to fare well in a recession, he may have the cash and be able to buy property, but it is a medium to long-term event and the ability to sustain the business model is only as good as the timing.

In the 1970s, with hyper-inflation and rising property prices in the UK, any property developer could create wealth, and this was to be repeated in the 10 years between 1997 and the recent property crash in 2007. There was easy credit made available to more than should have had it, which fuelled the property price rises and the result was the crash.

Returning to the data within the 1,000 referred to in the Sunday Times Rich List, the analysis by sector is also interesting and actually only shows one standard deviation from the norm for most categories.

Property and land	192
Finance	185
Industry	129
Film, arts, music, sport and media	84
Retail	73
Computers, telecoms, internet	65
Food and drink, retail and production	64
Leisure, hotels and travel	48
Construction	40
Business services and recruitment	32
Pharmaceuticals and health	29
Car sales and wholesaling	28
Transport, shipping and aviation	28
Lottery	3

So of 1,000 entrants across 15 categories, you would expect 71 in each category. Given that 238 have inherited their wealth and are therefore second or even third generation, to analyse the entrepreneurs and get a feel for industry sector let's look at the standard deviation.

The standard deviation is 56, so for one deviation each side of the mean, the range is 127 to 15. On the low side, this excludes lottery winners, hardly surprising.

On the high side we exclude those in property and land, which are almost certainly inherited. Also a close second is finance, along with 'industry', which seems to require closer analysis. As the range of one standard deviation (127 to 15) includes every other category, as the range marked includes all those categories with 84 to 28 entrants, which is clearly well within one standard deviation either side of the mean, then it seems that once you have made it into the 'big time', it does not matter what sector you are in.

This is principally because the range covers categories for everyone who has 'made it' to a certain degree and also because throughout the world we need something of everything and there will be big players in all industries. Trends over a period will dictate which industries develop and provide the wealth and growth.

It is worth reiterating again that our analysis is not of the richest and most successful entrepreneur, but of the ordinary entrepreneur, in general. The above analysis is to give an indication that you can make good in anything or any sector.

£££ OUR SURVEY ASKED...

Do you consider you are in the right sector?
92% said yes

If so, please mark its importance to where you are now, out of ten.
This scored a mark of 7.91

Surely this is a self-unfulfilling answer. Not everyone can be in the right sector.

The right sector at the right time is critical.

But it follows that as well as being in the right sector at any time, success is down to the entrepreneur to make it work. You can be in any sector at the right time and the timing may carry the less able entrepreneur to success.

CHAPTER THREE

FACTORY FITTED EXTRAS

3.1 Introduction

We have already analysed the intelligence and psyche of the entrepreneur and identified some basic tenets that go towards their make-up. However, how do they use these, and what character traits do they possess?

The entrepreneur does not sit in the back seat. They are not led but maintain their position as a leader and driver. Also, they have a vision that drives them forward and enables them to clearly see the end game. This section explores those elements and identifies what differentiates them from others. The leader generally has charisma.

This section will allow you to select the right person to sit in the driver's seat, someone who will best manipulate the controls around them.

3.2 The range of characters

Many management theories cover the role types within an organisation. To put any team together it is important to have individual strengths and differences in attitude so that the team develops and bonds and individuals can recognise and empathise with the individual egos therein. A cricket team of eleven wicketkeepers would be weak, but a good wicketkeeper in a team is vital.

The team is vital but what character does our entrepreneur possess?

£££ OUR SURVEY ASKED

Rank the following characteristics in order:

	Average rank in order out of 7
Leadership	5.0
Hard-working	4.5
Free thinking	4.2
Hungry/needs must	3.8
Courageous	3.6
Inventive	3.5
Risk-taking	3.4

Leadership came out first followed closely by being hard-working. Risk taking is last.

£££ OUR SURVEY ASKED...

For some 'free format' answers about the characteristic of an entrepreneur and sample answers were:

- Confident and responsible
- Integrity
- Decisive
- Determined and ever confident despite the odds
- Single minded
- Future focused and visionary

These are very different to the seven fixed answers, however decisiveness, determination and single mindedness are attributes or character traits we can recognise in any leader.

The most celebrated analysis of character traits and dynamics in business is probably Dr Belbin and his team roles.

These are generally used to identify people's behavioural strengths and weaknesses in the workplace. The definition of team roles, as stated by Dr Belbin, are:

> 'a tendency to behave, contribute and interrelate with others in a particular way'

So how does our entrepreneur fit in and what does he do to make his role effective in the group? The interpersonal skills ranked so highly in the previous chapter need to be put to good use in a team environment.

The roles that Belbin has defined are used widely throughout a number of organisations, but none of them clearly demonstrate the 'leader'. A few have that specific role in their brief, but is our entrepreneur a leader? This direct question is an interesting and relevant enquiry.

Let us review the reasons for team analysis so that we can see why it is so important. It is used to:

- Build productive working relationships in a business

- Select and develop high-performing teams

- Raise self-awareness and personal development

- Build mutual trust and understanding

- Aid recruitment processes

All of these are important for the entrepreneur.

Does the entrepreneur need to fall into any of these 'types' if they have the ideas and the drive to create their company? The answer is probably not, but they do need to use this theory to create the team to assist them. Also surely the entrepreneur has to be a team player, too. So they have to be within this group somewhere.

During the research Dr Belbin found that each team member was essential to the success of the team as a whole. The key was balance. For example, a 'Plant' is required to create an idea for the team to develop and push forward, but a team full of 'Plants' will produce lots of good ideas but some of which are most likely to be non-starters.

Also, with no 'Shaper' the team ambles along, but with too many 'Shapers' in-fighting will begin.

At this point it is worth analysing the roles to see if the entrepreneur or perhaps, the 'Chairman' is evident. In Belbin's first analysis of these roles, the Chairman did exist. There were only eight roles in existence. The 'Chairman's' role was then changed to the 'Co-ordinator' and a ninth, the 'Specialist', has been added. Both of these are effectively entrepreneurial.

It is natural to think of the founding entrepreneur as being the 'Chairman' but clearly they could be any of the roles, but may seek out the 'Chairman' or 'Co-ordinator' roles as they develop the seed of their business into a full-blown enterprise with staff, possibly for example with many branches and hopefully success.

Role	Gift to Team	Accepted Weakness
Co-ordinator	Mature, confident, identifies talent, clarifies goals, delegates effectively.	Could be seen as manipulative, offloads own share of the work
Plant	Creative, imaginative, free-thinking. Generates ideas and solves difficult problems.	Ignores incidental, too preoccupied to communicate effectively
Specialist	Single-minded, self-starter and dedicated. Provides knowledge and skills in rare supply.	Contributes only on a narrow front. Dwells on technicalities.
Shaper	Challenging dynamic, thrives on pressure. Has the drive and courage to overcome obstacles.	Prone to provocation. Offends people's feelings.

Resource Investigator	Outgoing and enthusiastic, communicative. Explores opportunities, develops contacts.	Over-optimistic, loses interest once initial enthusiasm has passed.
Completer Finisher	Painstaking, conscientious, anxious. Searches out errors. Polishes and perfects.	Inclined to worry unduly. Reluctant to delegate.
Team-worker	Co-operative, perceptive and diplomatic. Listens and averts friction.	Indecisive in crunch situations. Avoids confrontation.
Implementer	Practical, reliable, efficient. Turns ideas in to actions and organises work that needs to be done	Somewhat inflexible. Slow to respond to new possibilities.
Monitor Evaluator	Sober, strategic and discerning. Sees all the options and judges accurately.	Lacks drive and ability to inspire others. Can be overly critical.

This list is compiled in a specific order.

Clearly those roles at the top of the list are more likely to fit the entrepreneur as we have discovered already. The roles at the bottom of the list are clearly team roles, for team players who need the entrepreneur to lead them and develop the 'outer casing' and structure to a business.

Not many people can actually handle the outside pressures of dealing with...

- Over indulgent customers

- Unsupportive suppliers

- Annoying landlords

- Difficult staff issues

… all occurring at possibly the same time.

The quiet life with no difficulties or change is the prerequisite for the 'completer finisher', the 'team-worker', the 'implementer' and 'monitor evaluator'.

It is clear where that group of four, in particular, will fall down in an entrepreneurial situation, based on their weaknesses. Notwithstanding that they are very important in the team, they do not have the strength of character to be an entrepreneur.

The 'resource investigator' and 'shaper' can be entrepreneurs due to their dynamism and enthusiasm but they may almost certainly be prone to failure for losing sight of sense and practicalities around them.

The top three are our most likely source for the entrepreneur in the team.

The 'specialist' because they will arrive with the new product, service, idea or invention. They will provide detailed knowledge and workings of the product and probably industry knowledge too.

The 'plant' is creative and free-thinking and again, like the specialist, will be dynamic and creative in the business environment. This entrepreneur will 'spice up' any idea to hopefully make it a commercial and viable venture.

The 'co-ordinator' or 'chairman' will clarify goals. The art here is to cut to the chase and deliver on time. Delegation and identifying needs and talent are key to success.

All three are worthless as entrepreneurs without strong and effective communication skills. The three types above need to be rounded and need to smooth their accepted weaknesses in to strengths.

It is important to note that Belbin was creating a team for an effective organisation. We are creating the analysis of one person, the entrepreneur. How they fit into the team is important. Belbin saw that an individual has a dual role, their own skills and those skills used within a team environment.

Each of the team players have what we can call 'accepted weaknesses'. Where the removal of a weakness impacts on the effectiveness of an individual's strengths, then they are termed 'acceptable'.

£££ OUR SURVEY ASKED...

...to mark out of 10 the following characteristics that are required in the make up of an entrepreneur.

	The average mark in order was
Can make the really tough decisions	7.7
Strategic thinker	7.6
Single minded	7.3
Extrovert	5.9
Does not suffer fools	5.7
Ruthless	3.2
Bombastic	2.3

This clearly shows that the tough decisions, single mindedness and strategic thinking are the clear traits required in the make-up of an entrepreneur.

They are also the traits of a leader with charisma and possibly an extrovert who, because they know their own mind, does not suffer those around them if they do not perform. They are not to be read as ruthless and without heart. Integrity and compassion have featured heavily in the answers provided by entrepreneurs surveyed.

Ordinarily any entrepreneur would or should be considered the 'Chairman' or the leader of the team or business. In today's world the term Chairman may be considered politically incorrect so this has been altered to 'coordinator'. The new name actually fits the role better.

The coordinator is the one who presides over the team and ensures external goals and targets are set, put together in a coherent structure and (hopefully) achieved. This is a role naturally suited to the entrepreneur. Coordinators are distinguished for their focus on meeting objectives and the ability to include all team members.

They often display charisma and hold natural people skills. They are dominant but in a relaxed and unassertive way. They are not domineering and may tend towards manipulative behaviour. The co-ordinator will trust people unless there is strong evidence not to do so and are free of jealousy. All of these traits it is clear manifest themselves in an entrepreneur.

The coordinator is intelligent but not in any sense brilliant and is not a creative thinker. It is often thought rare that creative idea will come from such a person, albeit the entrepreneur will usually be creative, so the co-ordinator role will be only one, minor, aspect of the entrepreneur's character.

The pure co-ordinator will have the ability to bring out the best in each team member, focussing on their individual strong points. They will be conscious of using the team's combined strengths. They will establish work boundaries identify gaps and take steps to ensure they are filled.

The coordinator will find communication easy. As a result, setting objectives, and agendas, as well as taking responsibility for priorities and consultation, will be second nature. Leadership is all about this and this skill will make the entrepreneur easy to work for and successful in his own right. The contribution from the entrepreneur as a pure co-ordinator will be limited to this, and yet they could be just the right leader to raise money, handle public relations, deal with difficult negotiations and/or be an excellent figurehead.

Offloading their share of the work could be seen as a shirking of duties and manipulative, so could create divisions. But intelligent team members should soon realise someone has to do the 'dirty work'.

The 'specialist' meanwhile has a role that is second to none in the business. The entrepreneur is himself perhaps the specialist in the industry sector or the product and may know the product backwards, such that the business can only fail if he overdoes the detail and does not make the venture commercially viable. If the entrepreneur as a 'specialist' cannot see the wider picture he will need all of his coordinator skills to do so. A narrowness of vision will result in failure. Specialisms can be bought in, but there is nothing like having it in-house, for intellectual property and patent reasons as well as pure knowledge and possessing the cutting edge.

Creating good ideas and problem-solving is the role of the 'plant'. Communicating these ideas and remaining focused on them would be the plant's weakness and they need to rely on their co-ordinator instincts to win the day.

One of the best ways to start any entrepreneurial business is to have an effective and inspirational idea. The 'plant' provides those seeds. The plant is usually the most imaginative as well as the most intelligent member of the team. They are most likely to start searching for a new approach to a problem or issue. Plants are ordinarily much more concerned with major issues and fundamental concerns than with details. Indeed they are liable to ignore details and do need managing, hence the need for a strong co-ordinator. Originality of ideas, which border on radical, will come from the plant.

Surprisingly the plant, with their radical approach, is an extrovert – a characteristic most similar to the entrepreneur. Their insensitivity may not make them the best team member and therefore the overarching skill of the co-ordinator as a communicator will be needed, yet again. The 'plant' may not accept criticism well, and therefore the entrepreneur who is a plant will come across as single-minded to the extent of arrogance. The plant is vital to a project which is becoming ineffective and therefore is vital to the lifeblood of an organisation.

These are the three overriding team member character traits which suit our entrepreneur. A mix of 'coordinator', 'plant' and /or 'specialism' makes the perfect entrepreneur. The other skills can be hired. These three skills could be hired, however, to possess the necessary drive, vision and communication within an organisation and to have it positioned at its highest point, as the leader or Chairman would be a fatal flaw.

To finalise examining the character type of the entrepreneur, it is worth understanding character types portrayed in fiction, and particularly in the realms of comedy. It is in comedy that extremes are found. Our entrepreneur is not the 'loveable loser', nor the 'dumb one' or the 'womaniser' (until successful) but they can be the 'bitch or bastard' and sometimes 'in their own world or self-centred'. They may be 'neurotic' but they are almost certainly the 'logical and smart one' and definitely the 'materialistic one', once successful. However, the entrepreneur should not be not as a comedic personality as surely they may be demanding and on the take, rather than 'on the make'.

Frasier Crane was neurotic in both Cheers and Frasier – he could possibly be an entrepreneur (refer to the obsessive nature of the entrepreneur). The materialistic ones are best described by the demanding women in Cheers such as Rebecca and Diane, and perhaps Rachel in Friends. So not entrepreneurial in this instance, but wannabes.

Jerry Seinfield was the logical, smart one in the series of his own name Seinfield.

The characteristics of the logical and smart one would be:

- Articulate and well-spoken

- Balanced and brutally honest, patient

- Calm, caring and compassionate

- Grounded with common sense, stable

- Intelligent and knowledgeable

- Rational and reasonable

- Responsible and parental

- Sensible, smart, straightforward

From these clear character traits, our entrepreneur is born.

The entrepreneur as logical and smart and can make tough decisions, standing by and owning them. They can be a strategic thinker with clear vision. They are single-minded with energy and drive.

3.3 There's only one ego

The entrepreneur's ego is an important part of the title of this book and an important part of the entrepreneur, as the ego is paramount to their thinking and approach to business. It may be thought that ego might get in the way or cloud their judgement. Certainly not.

£££ OUR SURVEY ASKED...
Rather than taking risks, do you back your own judgement?
100% answered Yes

If so, then please mark out of ten how confident you are of your own ability?
The mark achieved was 8.16

This is the only mark that obtained a 100% result. It is extraordinary to think EVERY entrepreneur questioned said yes, to this question. There is no deviation – they all have confidence in themselves. This is not demonstrating arrogance. It is self-belief.

This self-belief is evident and at the heart of almost every decision he makes. Self-belief must not turn in to self-interest.

Self-interest can overtake reasoned judgement when someone with that trait is making decisions. An example may be the decision that an investment in a new website is less important than the cost of the next holiday. The choice becomes personal expenditure over the well-being of the business and its own sustainability suffers as a direct result.

£££ OUR SURVEY ASKED...
Does the fear of failure drive you?
64% said yes
36% said no

The entrepreneur will generally put the business ahead of himself. Responsible and reasoned judgement will be evident.

This is a fair comment for entrepreneurs who consider that proof of their success is the trappings that money can buy. Their ego is satisfied by some psychopathological desire to spend, show off and brazenly manifest wealth in a materialistic manner.

Often, it is not wealth that purchases the nice car, yacht or holiday home, but borrowed money on an unsustainable business model. The wealth is shown as a badge of honour. It is somewhat sad, as those days are outdated. Credit has been so easy that Joe average drives a nice car, but we are probably talking about Ferraris and Porsches.

Everyone knows that it is nice to drive a nice car, a comfortable car and one which does not go wrong and is reliable. A car of your choice is important. However, the most expensive cars are hardly the prizes of successful entrepreneurs. They may be for those who have sold, (please see Section 7 'trade in'), but the most expensive and fuel-thirsty vehicles are the toys of playboys and 'a listers'. These cars are not tax efficient and not the easiest to drive through congested city traffic. They are play-things and should be kept as such.

These are the words of a protestant businessperson but they make sense. Practicality rules the day. The customers and suppliers of the entrepreneur would approve of efficient but comfortable motoring.

The ego needs handling but it can be easily satisfied with a nice car. The expensive car should stay in the garage.

Every strong character will undoubtedly have an ego. It will be most evident if the entrepreneur is arrogant. However they will suffer as they will not engage with customers and employees and their interpersonal skills will be weak. So successful entrepreneurs do not have such arrogance and if they do, they suppress it.

This could take the form of being, perhaps, an industry expert or specialist as per the character type referred to above. The ego needs harnessing into a responsible and reliable person who can carry the weight of the business and an understanding the needs of others.

Other unacceptable forms of ego include always considering your approach or view to be correct. This again is self destructive. Unless the entrepreneur is always correct, they will inevitably make a poor judgement, and the venture will fail. The conceited nature of this approach will get in the way of listening and taking advice.

An ego is required in the life of hard knocks. The ego is important, and quite honestly, it is vital to any entrepreneur's success.

The knock may come in the form of:

- A patent or idea not being protected and being copied, resulting in legal battles

- Competition which takes away employees, customers or locations

- Anything which distracts the entrepreneur from the job in hand and takes away their focus from the strategy

- Unreasonable customer demands

- Inability to raise money, and excessive time being taken on such matters, albeit it is important

- An employee or team leaving with part of the business and setting up or with a competitor

- Machinery failure

- Act of God' without adequate insurance

- Inadequate insurance covering every eventuality even professional indemnity.

If any of these occur, specifically in say, the first two years of a business the entrepreneur may not know who to turn to and will need to ensure that they are hardened or have a big enough ego to deal with the issue and resolve it. The resolution is for the success of their venture, to safeguard their investment and the investors, customers and employees who have placed their trust in them to deliver.

£££ OUR SURVEY ASKED...

Do you generally discuss big decisions with others, as a sounding board?

80% said yes, they did

The entrepreneur knows where to turn when they need to discuss decisions. They will be strong a strategic thinker, but will take advice and seek others' views – an excellent trait with such an ego.

So, the entrepreneur has to be extremely focussed, able to deal with extraordinary events hitting them and their business, which they cannot take personally unless of course, they continually put themselves or their business at risk by allowing situations to grow and fester.

This hardness or ability to cope is required at all times, not only if one problem occurs, but if there are multiple issues. In other words, the entrepreneur has to understand where they have to get to, and get there, notwithstanding outside events or 'knocks'. This is what is described as driven. It can, as well, be misunderstand and considered single -minded, which suggests an element of selfishness.

Being driven is a key characteristic of the working class and immigrants. Both of these classes have to find housing, shelter, food and clothing for themselves and their family, sometimes in hardship and, as mentioned above for the immigrant on foreign shores, in a foreign language with a foreign culture.

Therefore it is hardly surprising that a large number of successful entrepreneurs may be first or second generation immigrants. They possess the drive to survive.

They are not given any hand outs and it can often be said that families move from 'riches to rags to riches' in three generations. The first generation makes the money, the second wastes it and the third has to overcome that loss and make it again.

Eastern European immigrants in America would chant: 'For frying, for baking, for cooking. Good also for eating, herring will do for every meal, and for every class.'

A statistic for the future will be that the white indigenous people of the UK made up 94.1% of the population and in the 1991 census it dropped to 86% in 2011. Will the business leaders be from the minority non-indigenous population in the future, as the indigenous population sit back and take the spoils of the education, job security and culture that they know so well, indulging in the drinking and welfare culture?

Demographic change can lead to a shortage of opportunities, but in the mind of the driven, focused entrepreneur, this becomes an opportunity in itself. The great depression in the 1930s proved this without doubt, as the statistics showed in 1910 there were 30.1 births per 1,000 of the population, dropping in 1935 to 18.7 then rising to nearly 40.0 in the 1990s. A low birth rate means more opportunity as there will be less competition and then more opportunity in time as the birth rate picks up creating younger members of the population to consume the goods generated.

So the entrepreneur is driven to their position, not by their intelligence or character traits but by their determination, and often without funds for their venture. Therefore, undoubtedly, they have to take risks.

Entrepreneurs need an 'ego', it is how it evidences itself, that is important.

3.4 Taking risks

Any business requires funding and the start-up funding whether by debt or equity is required to finance those first costs. They may be materials for a product, to pay the first month's wages or the costs of the premises from which to operate, and perhaps even for deposits to buy plant and equipment.

A well thought-out business plan and strategy will account for the initial costs and set-up costs as described above, as well as the working capital required for the first three or six months or even a year until the business is self-sustainable.

The source of this initial capital is the dilemma for the entrepreneur.

£££ OUR SURVEY ASKED...
Did you start with:

Your own money	64%
Support from friends and family	16%
Bank funding	13%
Venture capital	11%
No money	33%
Other	7%

One answer from 'Other' related to the support and upfront payment from a customer. What a good way to start! The risk of putting finance in to a small or new venture is probably the hardest decision any entrepreneur has to make.

So where does the immigrant potential entrepreneur obtain this capital? Would they be part of the 33% with no money. Probably.

It is not always easily generated from savings, nor is it available from the bank of 'Mum and Dad', or even 'Grandad and Grandma', perhaps.

'Investment readiness' is a term now used for small businesses to understand and benefit from further support to turn their idea, notion or inception of a business into a real venture and attract investors, even if it is as simple as a bank overdraft. Securing funding can be closely related to how well a business makes itself ready for this potential investment for example how attractive it is to fund.

Initial seed investment often comes from friends and family. It can come from savings or even, as many immigrants do, venture in a very small way. Think of Jack Cohen of Tesco's, his start was very small, it became successful, not overstepping the mark, by controlling overhead and making profit which generated cash which was then always reinvested. That is not always the case.

Spending your savings or life savings or even a redundancy payment has risk. It is easy to risk £100 if have a further £1,000 in the bank but not so easy to risk £100 if you have £1 in the bank. Just as much as poverty or immigration can focus the mind with hunger and result in drive and focus, so can the act of borrowing money.

The initial capital is called seed capital, and friends and family may provide the funding, if not the entrepreneur themselves.

The advantages would be:

- low or zero interest

- no need for security nor dilution of equity

- a longer period before the lender expects repayment or a return

- greater flexibility

- a less detailed business plan.

All of these are 'warm and friendly' and hardly commercial, with strict commercial constraints, unless of course the funds are raised by borrowing against an asset external to the business such as a mortgage on the entrepreneur's own home, but that should be classed as borrowing despite those funds entering the business as equity.

The weaknesses are clear. The funding may fall short of real need. The lack of a commercially viable business plan may lead to unforeseen mistakes in the business model. Unless the business goes to plan, then unnecessary friction will ensue between the entrepreneur and the financier as the entrepreneur will need yet more support.

Some of the best results are made on or from borrowed funds. The concept of borrowing is fundamental to convincing someone else, probably a professional, that the business or venture has legs. It can last long enough to repay the initial capital borrowed and the cost of borrowing that capital.

Borrowing does focus the mind. It can be a worry, if wanton and uncontrolled.

Equally a lender would like to see some commitment from the entrepreneur, not only a commitment in terms of money invested, perhaps matching the investor, but also demonstrated by extracting a wage less than would ordinarily be appropriate. This is to enable the business to get onto a proper footing and take away one of the leading reasons for failure. This is, if you recall, the extraction of funds by the entrepreneur that the business cannot afford. So certain constraints will be put on the business by the lender. Quite rightly.

The idea of being watched over by external investors or lenders, and of having external debts, often puts entrepreneurs off borrowing. This is hardly so, if the strategy is sound. The business will become self-sustainable and prove its own worth quickly.

Debt finance is generally short-term and allows entrepreneurs to retain 100% of their business. This is attractive and may also reduce the time and effort required to raise the finance compared to equity, as the finance is purely focused on the restricted requirement for the asset itself.

Leasing and renting assets such as plant, equipment and even premises are most favourable. These items do not need short-term capital or long-term capital either. Most providers of such finance secure against the particular asset. On occasions the entrepreneur will have to give a personal guarantee but this would only be to the value of the debt itself and may not be as onerous if the asset holds its value and creates equity which could on sale settle the debt.

The advantages would be:

- terms and amount are tailored to need and are quicker to arrange

- repayments are planned and the impact on cash flow budgeted, with interest affordable

- there is tax relief on the interest paid

- the terms, especially if an overdraft are regularly reviewed.

The disadvantages may be that unless adequate security is forthcoming the lender may be reluctant to lend to a new or start up business. The shorter the term, the more expensive, and of course the overdraft is repayable on demand and there may be different personnel or view taken on renewal. The entrepreneur needs to read that situation ahead of time and renew say for a longer period over a time of relative difficulty. However, that relates to the logical and smart entrepreneur. Vision has yet to be covered.

Penalties on default can count heavily against the future credit rating of the business. The entrepreneur, if this were to occur, would not be able to relate to the lender and particularly the career banker, with their fixed view, looking over their shoulder at their manager, and with the underwriter in the background, all seeking long-term careers and good pension packages from their employers. There would not be a natural meeting of minds. The free-thinking optimistic entrepreneur would be frustrated with the 'jobs worth' financier.

During a recession, when businesses perform badly there are often tales of entrepreneurs distrusting banks who have not given the entrepreneur enough time to trade through the lean times. This is the subject of a much longer piece on funding but fits well with the ego of the entrepreneur getting in the way of common sense and not seeing that their business model needs to change, be updated or is just outdated and does not work anymore.

The business model needs constant review. How does the entrepreneur keep the business fresh, meet customer demand and service? These questions allow the entrepreneur to find the right market successfully invest external funding, and therefore reduce risk.

The production of a business plan is considered by many as an unnecessary, expensive and time-consuming exercise. The considered, professional view is that it brings everything together. The business plan demonstrates strategy. It should demonstrate where any risk lies.

Most importantly, it codifies the entrepreneur's thinking. It should show clearly the financial plan will (in almost 100% of cases) show a profit and most importantly when it will do so. This often is shown to be earlier than it will actually occur. The ego will create optimism and potentially some unreality within the plan. Unless, of course, the plan is written so conservatively that it is not worth investing. The plan while showing a strategy needs to show reality.

The information in the plan (outlined below) will be in summary form, supported by well thought-out detail. The sections below would be written over a number paragraphs supported by commentary and spreadsheets.

- An executive summary, details of key people, market research, the marketing and sales plan.

- The financial information showing historic data (if applicable) and assumptions to develop the future prospects.

- The forecast profit and loss account – in summary and supported in detail, by product, branch, market etc

- Importantly, the forecast cash-flow and balance sheets, with sensitivities

- Details of the requirement for asset purchases, re-investment and capital, together with interest cover and payback.

The financial data above would show as and when external capital is required and the likely source and exposure.

The right type of finance is essential. It needs to match the need for the finance.

Short-term finance is generally to fund working capital, and this can take the form of bank overdraft or other debtor book financing and will come with attachments and be relatively expensive. Unless a short term loan from the owner or otherwise this would almost always be debt.

Medium-term finance is essentially to fund assets with a relatively short life or those which may last three to five years. This is generally a mixture between debt or equity.

Long-term finance is to last the length and life of the business, almost certainly. This will be relatively cheap, if not receive payment on reward and therefore share the business' risks. This is ordinarily equity based.

Therefore the finance splits neatly between equity and debt.

Equity matches the long term and/or medium term and is rarely short term. Debt would be long term if it is a term loan and security would be required because its only payback is the initial capital and interest. Rarely would a premium attach.

Equity finance is suitable for those 'joining in the journey'. This is a little bit of a hackneyed expression, but expresses exactly what is meant by the form of finance. Equity finance will receive their coupon in the way of dividend as and when the business can afford it, and it should not put the business at risk. It will also receive its full pay out if the business is sold successfully. These are the riches on offer. See the section on 'trade-in'. However some entrepreneurs may believe that the business is possibly worth more than it is actually is, and need to groom their business for sale. Again their ego may deflect this, but the sensible entrepreneur will groom the business for sale and jump off the treadmill as the business outgrows them. More importantly they may feel that they need to handover to more experienced industrial professionals. It is not just about retirement – there will be much more on this subject later.

Risk is attached to the method of finance.

FFE OUR SURVEY ASKED...

Are there other reasons, in your view, that businesses may fail?

The answers were:
- Cash flow
- Not understanding the cost structure
- Unrealistic business plan and over-optimism
- Too much involvement with internal matters
- Lack of ambition and understanding customer needs
- No intentions in the company aligned
- Not making tough decisions
- Trailblazing for competitors benefits
- Too much reliance on one customer
- Lack of adaptability
- And cash flow........again and again

Equity finance can be sourced from business angels individually or syndicated, venture capital houses and private equity. Companies and businesses have grown into this space and offer the necessary finance.

Many would-be entrepreneurs look at this as a form of debt but the smart businessperson who receives equity finance may decide to receive the finance alongside the input of an 'industry experienced' board member. Extra finance can be raised to fund an acquisition or merger or as a stepping stone to become a larger organisation and possible exit.

Equity finance performs a number of other roles apart from just giving the business standing. It creates a market for its worth, just as letting out part of a property does. It shows a real worth and a value intrinsic in the business.

The main advantages of equity finance are:

- the funding is committed to the business

- the right partner can be invaluable

- investors have a direct interest in its success and can act as a guide

- investors are often available for a second round of funding and their participation may lead others to invest as well – join the club!

The disadvantages would be that the raising of such equity can be demanding, time- consuming and expensive. It may bring certain legal and reporting duties to the otherwise free-thinking entrepreneur. The activity itself may distract from the actual business. The business case would be under severe scrutiny and as a result could encroach on the entrepreneur's ego. Major strategic decisions would then be subject to greater review and, at an early stage of the life of the business, the business may suffer from being somewhat inflexible.

It is worth noting that the new internet age has provided an alternative. Crowd funding using social media platforms can raise capital through a large number of investors each contributing a relatively small amount of money. As this is written crowd funding looks quick and easy, fun, cheap and available but as yet unregulated.

Perhaps most importantly the dilution of the owner's share may reduce the entrepreneur's drive and hunger to such an extent they lose their sharp edge. The sharp edge and focus is essential and critical to success. If there is risk and the entrepreneur is 'up for taking that risk' then they need the rewards too. Why share them – within reason?

There are many equity-funding innovations and from time to time government intervention allows these, with certain tax reliefs.

It is down to the entrepreneur to reduce his risk.

£££ OUR SURVEY ASKED...

Do you think that you take risks?
79% said yes

The importance of risking-taking to getting the entrepreneur to where they are now was scored:
6.75 out of 10

Generally the entrepreneur will relish the risk and challenge, and any problem could and should be overcome, but they will need adequate professional advice. Seek it at the right time and listen and act on it.

£££ OUR SURVEY ASKED...

	% saying yes
Have you considered employing a chairman?	39%
Do you employ a chairman?	21%
Do you wish you had more finance in the business?	44%
Have you sought external finance?	47%
Do you recognise any weaknesses in yourself	96%
Have you compensated for those weaknesses?	72%

This is a fairly honest assessment that the entrepreneur does not know everything, they may know their own mind but will seek assistance when required. They will also recognise and work on in their weaknesses. While optimism is a necessary trait alongside drive, realism has to be evident.

The entrepreneur needs to make the most of all of the talent that is available to reduce risk.

They need to ensure that they receive payment leading to healthy cash flow. They need to protect and identify patents, copyright or technology.

Reducing risk is the key to success, but having the drive and strength of character to take it on the first instance is perhaps even more fundamental. The entrepreneur is certainly an interesting character. They are surely becoming very worthy of their riches, once successful.

The accepted understanding has been that entrepreneurs have a greater tolerance for risk compared to others. Hence the riskier-than-normal steps they take to seek those riches. While conventional wisdom assumes entrepreneurs have great risk tolerance within a controlled analysis that tracks attitudes, it was consistently found that they were not that different, in fact could be risk-averse.

Entrepreneurs do not like risks that cannot be controlled. However, they are very confident in their own ability. In that respect they are above the average. Hence they take risk and seek success but based on their own ability. If asked to choose between two situations, one which requires a high level of ability and uncertainty and the other a low level of ability and uncertainty the entrepreneur will choose the first because of (over) confidence in their own ability. This must not be confused with arrogance.

This book has covered differences in education, culture, social environment and family tradition in parts, but it is confidence that drives the entrepreneur.

Over-confidence encourages the entrepreneur to engage in an uncertain industry. The entrepreneur is then rewarded with success for taking such risky measures, and seeking and following the required advice. But the rewards forthcoming for the luck and work involved in reaching that success in that riskier setting need to be high.

£££ OUR SURVEY ASKED...
Do you feel that successful entrepreneurs should stick to what they know?
48% said yes
52% said no

This is a very neutral answer.

The entrepreneur backs their own judgement and their integrity is such that where they can they will do their utmost to repay the debt which they take on, responsibly. They do not see debt as risk.

Riskier individuals would certainly diversify and enter into unknown markets and that debt to fund that activity is risky.

3.5 Reaping the rewards

The 'Ragged-Trousered Philanthropists' was first published in 1914. It was written by Robert Tressell. His only book, he died soon after he finished it in 1911, and never witnessed its success.

Roy Hattersley (deputy leader of the Labour party from 1983-92) wrote a wonderful synopsis of this amazing story in the New Statesman in February 2011. He started by saying that 'Robert Tressell was guilty of the sin of despair' and finished by admitting that 'the importance [of the book] was the emphasis it places on the need to change the whole social system. Its weakness is its assumption that the working class is too craven and corrupt to work gradually towards achieving that end.'

The novel has had many plaudits and reviewers, none other than George Orwell who acclaimed that the book was 'the first to put the facts of working class life...onto paper'. It was in effect responsible for a paradigm shift in consciousness. The Times Literary Supplement felt that the book told the reader 'more about the rise of the British Labour party its instincts, traditions and future than all the fireworks of Bernard Shaw or the blueprints of the Webbs.'

The reason that a snapshot review of this book is mentioned here is because capitalist theory and the entrepreneur is brought conspicuously and severely in to question in this work.

£££ OUR SURVEY ASKED...	% yes
Do you like the trappings of success?	88%
Do you aspire to more success and more of those trappings?	71%
Do you try and hide your wealth?	53%

Anyone reading this book by Robert Tressell today would think it was written last year or even the year before that. The fact that it was written over 100 years ago, and stands the test of time, is not a merit of the book but a damnation of the social system and the inability of the political classes to enable the 'working' classes to move forward with the times. Not only to move forward with the times, but to accept the role of the entrepreneur who through their endeavours brings the benefits they will give to society rather than to be despised as a taker and portraying selfishness.

As demonstrated above, 88% of entrepreneurs surveyed like the trappings of success and 71% want more. Conscious of society's jealousy, 53% of the same sample try to play their wealth down, but why should they?

We have yet to incur the full effects of the 'flattening' of society as a result of the new industrial revolution during the age of the internet and of knowledge for all, but surely the ability to immediately access any website anywhere in the world will have an impact on society. Regardless of whether this is considered good or bad, universal access to information will surely make it possible for anyone to climb the ladder. The word social is deliberately missed out, as that is not the ladder in question.

Entrepreneurs first emerged in Victorian, industrial England and 19th-century America (with its magnificent creation of wealth for the chosen few). They generated hatred because of their suppression of the worker and creditor. They did not know, nor recognise, any social responsibility.

£££ OUR SURVEY ASKED...
You can draw from your business and choose two of the following:

	In order, max 2
Pay off as much debt as you can	1.56
Give bonuses to the staff	0.44
Keep the money in the bank	0.36
Put a deposit down on an investment property	0.20
Buy an expensive car	0.20
Fund your pension	0.16
Treat the family to a holiday of a lifetime	0.08

This shows a responsible entrepreneur in our midst. Not only looking to pay off any debt but also rewarding key staff.

The 'Ragged-Trousered Philanthropists' contains a wonderful passage transcribed here, where Owen, a mysterious journeyman-prophet with a strange vision of a just society joins a group of English working class people. He wins their trust slowly and rouses them from their dour and dull complacency with spirited attacks on greed and dishonesty, which he maintains are the fundamentals of the corrupt capitalist system.

" 'Money is the real poverty,' said Owen.

'Prove it,' repeated Crass

'Money is the cause of poverty because it is the device by which those who are too lazy to work are enabled to rob the workers of the fruits of their labours.'

'Prove it,' said Crass

Owen slowly folded up the piece of newspaper he had been reading and put it into his pocket.

'All right,' he replied' I'll show you how the Great Money Trick is worked.'

Owen opened his dinner basket and took from it two slices of bread but as these were not sufficient, he requested that anyone who had some bread left would give it to him. They gave him several pieces which he placed in a heap on a clean piece of paper, and, having borrowed the pocket knives they used to cut and eat their dinners with from Easton, Harlow and Philpot, he addressed them as follows:

'These pieces of bread represent the raw materials which exist naturally in and on the earth for the use of mankind, they were not made by any human being, but were created by the Great Spirit for the benefit and sustenance of all, the same as were the air and the light of the sun.'

'You're about as fair-speakin' a man as I've met for some time,' said Harlow, winking at the others.

'Yes mate,' said Philpot. 'Anyone would agree to that much! It's as clear as mud.'

'Now' continued Owen, 'I am a capitalist; or, rather, I represent the landlord and capitalist class. That is to say, all these raw materials belong to me. It does not matter for our present argument how I obtained possession of them, or whether I have any legal right to them; the only thing that matters now is the admitted fact that all the raw materials which are necessary for the production of the necessaries of life are now the property of the Landlord and Capitalist class. I am that class: all these raw materials belong to me.'

'Good enough!' agreed Philpot.

'Now you three represent the Working Class: you have nothing – and for my part, although I have these raw materials, they are of no use to me – what I need is – the things that can be made out of these raw materials by Work: but as I am too lazy to work for myself, I have invented the Money Trick to make you work for me. But first I must explain that I possess something else beside the raw materials. These knives represent all the machinery of production: the factories, tools, railways and so forth, without which the necessaries of life cannot be produced in abundance. And these three coins' – taking three halfpennies from his pocket – 'represent my Money Capital.'

'But before we go any further,' said Owen, interrupting himself, 'it is most important that you remember I am not supposed to be merely "a" capitalist. I represent the whole Capitalist Class. You are not supposed to be just three workers – you represent the whole Working Class.'

'All right, all right,' said Crass impatiently, 'we all understand that. Git on with it.'

Owen proceeded to cut up one of the whole slices of bread into a number of little square blocks.

'These represent the things which are produced by labour, aided by machinery, from the raw materials. We will suppose that three of these blocks represent – a week's work. We will suppose that a weeks' work is worth – one pound: and we will suppose that each of these ha'pennies is a sovereign. We'd be able to do the trick better if we had real sovereigns, but I forgot to bring any with me.'

'I'd lend you some,' said Philpot regretfully, 'but I left me purse on our grand pianner.'

As by a strange coincidence nobody happened to have any gold with them, it was decided to make shift with the halfpence.

'Now this is the way the trick works – '

'Before you goes on with it interrupted Philpot, apprehensively, 'don't you think we'd better have someone to keep watch at the gate in case a Slop comes along? We don't want to get runned in, you know.'

I don't think there's any need for that,' replied Owen. 'There's only one slop who'd interfere with us for playing this game, and that's Police Constable Socialism.'

'Never mind about Socialism,' said Crass irritably. 'Get along with the bloody trick.'

Owen now addressed himself to the working classes as represented by Philpot, Harlow and Easton.

'You say you are all in need of employment, and as I am the kind-hearted capitalist class I am going to invest all my money in various industries, so as to give you Plenty of Work. I shall pay each of you one pound per week, and a week's work is – you must each produce three of these square blocks. For doing this work you will each receive your wages; the money will be your own, to do as you like with, and the things you produce will of course be mine, to do as I like with. You will each take one of these machines and as soon as you have done a week's work, you shall have your money.'

The Working Classes accordingly set to work, and the Capitalist class sat down and watched them. As soon as they had finished, they passed the nine little blocks to Owen who placed them on a piece of paper by his side and paid the workers their wages.

'These blocks represent the necessities of life. You can't live without some of these things, but as they belong to me, you will have to buy them from me: my price for these blocks is - one pound each.'

As the working classes were in need of the necessaries of life and as they could not eat drink or wear the useless money, they were compelled to agree to the kind Capitalist's terms. They each bought back and at once consumed one-third of the produce of their labour. The capitalist class also devoured two of the square blocks, and so the net result of the week's work was that the kind capitalist had consumed two pounds worth of the things produced by the labour of others, and reckoning the square at their market value of one pound each, he had more than double his capital, for he still possessed the three pounds in money and is addition four pounds worth of goods. As for the working classes, Philpot, Harlow and Easton, having each consumed the pound's worth of necessaries they had bought with their wages, they were again precisely in the same condition as when they started work – they had nothing.

This process was repeated several times; for each week's work the producers paid their wages. They kept on working and spending all their earnings. The kind-hearted capitalist consumed twice as much as any one of them and his pile of wealth continually increased. In a little while – reckoning the little squares at their market value of one pound each – he was worth about one hundred pounds, and the working classes were still in the same condition as when they began, and were still tearing into their work as if their lives depended upon it.

After a while the rest of the crowd began to laugh, and their merriment increased when the kind-hearted capitalist, just after having sold a pound's worth of necessaries to each of his workers, suddenly took their tools – the Machinery of Production – the knives away from, them, and informed them that as owing to Over Production at his store-houses were glutted with the necessaries of life, he had decided to close down the works.

'Well, and wot the bloody 'ell are we to do now?' demanded Philpot.

'That's not my business,' replied the kind hearted capitalist. 'I've paid you your wages, and provided you with Plenty of Work for a long time past. I have no more work for you to do at present. Come round again in a few month's time and I'll see what I can do for you.'

'But what about the necessaries of life?' demanded Harlow? 'We must have something to eat.'

'Of course you must,' replied the capitalist affably; 'and I shall be very pleased to sell you some.'

'But we ain't got no bloody money!'"

While this book maintains its roots in working class doctrine, this passage clearly demonstrates the anger, jealousy and obvious contempt for the capitalist class by the poor, down-trodden, abused and exploited worker. The book continues with its story.

The entrepreneur (or capitalist) is despised and given short shrift as the workers in this story try and deceive him and get away with short hours, shoddy work, for as much money as they can. The story continues showing how the working class cannot use that money properly and barely make enough to scrape by each week. Hence Hattersley's comments about that class, that they themselves cannot escape their 'lot' or the hand that life deals them.

This passage proves that the capitalist grows richer from the labour of the working man. This is enough to goad and rile those workers against the capitalist. The workers carry no risk, have no responsibility do not care where the market lies and the least of all the price or payment for the goods produced.

The worker works, the capitalist or entrepreneur worries, takes his work home with him and bears all the responsibility, for that alone, he should surely receive reward.

This is not a potted history of the period from 1900 to 1950, however it is worth noting that our inbred thoughts and doctrines have been formed during this period of post industrialisation by perhaps a conceited and greedy capitalist class.

FFE OUR SURVEY ASKED...

	% yes
Do you feel others are clearly jealous of you?	61%
Do you feel they understand the cost to you of being an entrepreneur?	21%
Would it be easier if you had a job and not your business?	25%

There is clearly jealousy, as well as a lack of understanding surrounding entrepreneurs. One in four said they felt the onus of carrying the business is too much – quite a frightening statistic. Health and happiness are not always derived from running a business.

The British Labour party was founded in 1900. By 1910, 42 Labour MPs were elected to the House of Commons. The early part of the 20th century saw a whole raft of reforms to improve the conditions of the working class. Flagship milestones for the masses under labour governments were The Wheatley Housing Act, providing 500,000 homes for rent, under Ramsey Macdonald. The creation of the National Health Service in 1947, under Clement Attlee and the beginnings of the welfare state as we know it, from the Beveridge report first published in December 1942, strangely during war time.

The Labour party was strongly aligned with, if not supported financially and by votes from, the trade union movement. By uniting, the workers formed enough strength to bargain for better pay, conditions and safety. These were not awarded incorrectly. It is inhumane to expect an ordinary working person to suffer during their work and become diseased and ravaged by ill health as some of their predecessors did.

So just as much as the worker needs to understand the benefits, which should be given by the responsible and successful entrepreneur, so must the entrepreneur provide market-based pay, as good conditions as he can afford, a safe environment and adequate training and supervision for his team.

We are moving from the terms of 'greedy capitalist' to successful entrepreneur, and from – 'exploited worker' to valuable team member.

On this basis, the relationship can prosper. It takes a maturity of thought and the provision of a belief in the political classes for everyone to think they can aspire to not only have a living wage but also perhaps one day becoming the entrepreneur themselves.

Being the entrepreneur as we discover takes a special person.

The special person has every right to earn the trappings of success, or spend company or business money as deemed appropriate, such as:

- A larger than necessary wage or salary

- The choice of structure of remuneration ie money and/or benefit

- The use of tax-efficient remuneration schemes

- The ability to choose how surplus profits are invested

- The building of nest eggs from surplus profits

- The choice of car

- The choice of pension and/or savings provision

- Use of company money for marketing and advertising budgets, which satisfy personal hobbies, why not?

- Employing friends or family

- Choice of suppliers

All the while, ensuring the business or venture has enough working capital to survive. This means not putting employees or suppliers at risk. Paying taxes as they fall due as a responsible person, should. Remember, one of the main reasons businesses fail is that reason alone. The financial benefits derived from the venture come last.

The entrepreneur who denies the company of working capital or money to invest and takes, is deluding themselves. There are many examples of remuneration or drawings being too high for the profits, let alone the re-investment required. This stifles the business of growth potential or ambition.

The employee trusts the entrepreneur such that he knows his wage is safe so that they will be paid, when it falls due. The suppliers trust they are to be paid and not 'knocked' or part-paid. Integrity and responsibility is fundamental.

Clearly, trust and track-record do count for an awful lot in an entrepreneur's early years, so the effort has a payback. The entrepreneur, if successful, should be able to financially benefit and as a result buy a car of their choice, even at list price and not second hand!

They should, without guilt, fund their wishes. Guilt would mean the entrepreneur funds his wishes ahead of others, who do not get paid as a result.

That is not the way the responsible entrepreneur operates.

CHAPTER FOUR

THE TEST DRIVE

4.1 Introduction

The entrepreneur, as strong-minded as they appear to be, will go their own way in creating their strategy and direction for their business.

However, the clever entrepreneur will listen to others with more experience and use various management techniques. This will be to not only fully develop their own capabilities where they feel they may have weaknesses but also to ensure the business and venture has every chance of success.

This section will discuss those techniques and relate them to the ego of the entrepreneur so that we can empathise and clearly understand their methods. This is when the car is running smoothly and going for its test drive. We need to measure and improve its performance and that of its driver.

4.2 The component parts

The entrepreneur will not be an expert in every business discipline.

The successful entrepreneur will recognise their deficiencies and correct these in a variety of ways.

In terms of a skill base a businessperson has four key areas to cover and these are:

Sales	Marketing
Operations	Administration

It is commonly held as an opinion that the successful entrepreneur will be competent and interested in at least three of these (if not three and a half). Being able to understand the skills and initiatives within each discipline and form considered opinions and contribute to the roles, albeit not necessarily being professionally trained in them nor understanding the finer points of each; the inner workings of each section of machinery in the plant, say.

£££ OUR SURVEY ASKED
Please order the skills in importance for an entrepreneur

	Score out of 5
Sales	3.4
Marketing	3.3
Inventiveness and creativity	2.9
Finance	2.8
Operations	2.7

The most interesting aspect of this answer is the grouping. There is a clear winner being, sales and marketing, but the grouping around the average 'three' is very obvious and clear. All the skills are considered equally as important.

The entrepreneur must be savvy enough to realise that the hours of downtime that a section of plant is out of operation are costly in many respects and need fixing. It means that operations cannot fulfil sales. This seems obvious and simple, but in the maelstrom of a hectic hour at the office, dealing with the production facility's problems may be forgotten. The plant must be maintained to keep such delays to a minimum. The operations manager has a vote at meetings. How often are certain procedural matters overlooked?

If the businessperson is unclear about the importance of administration, answering mail promptly, dealing with payments, compliance and taxation matters on a timely basis then they are not the complete entrepreneur that they maintain they are or aspire to. Keeping quality financial and management information is critical to success, as shown below reading the dashboard. Organisational prowess is key to the ability to deal with and prioritise matters.

So, each of the four functions make the business work well in unison and the entrepreneur thereby becomes successful when they do.

These functions can be improved by hiring suitably remunerated individuals who are expert and experienced in these areas. The skills of marketing, sales and operations, subject to say being a qualified finance professional, will generally rest with the entrepreneur.

The key for the entrepreneur is to then enhance their own management technique or understanding of the missing skills that will make their business work that much smoother, tick that bit louder and create clear and obvious market advantage.

They could undertake coaching.

> **£££** OUR SURVEY ASKED
> ### Do you read management books?
> 61% said yes

The entrepreneur will probably find this coaching a bore, an unproductive use of time and a chore unless it is delivered in small measures. The entrepreneur has little patience for fools and a clear vision of the path ahead, and to put endless courses in their way will only frustrate them.

A week on a senior management course, while:

- customers are screaming for delivery and

- operations need advice on priorities and

- accounts need direction on collections,

would not provide the entrepreneur with a free and an uncomplicated mind to learn. This is required by the entrepreneur to concentrate on the essential course and self-development. Quality time must be found.

OUR SURVEY ASKED

Do you go on management courses to develop yourself, your skill set and to self-educate?
48% said yes

This is actually a lower percentage than those reading management books, the earlier question, but 1 in 2 is still a relatively high answer and a distinct measure of the entrepreneur's awareness that self-improvement, particularly in areas where they are not skilled is paramount to their success. You never stop learning.

As important as the recruitment, management and encouragement of the team is, the unseen time spent on management of the business and cash flow to get to the end of each month is just as important. The day-to-day requirements to deliver the sales, collect the cash and pay the wages are essential.

More important is the overall strategy. This often takes a back seat, and is best addressed in down time or on weekends with a clear head.

Coaching and training on how the business should be run is not considered well-spent time for the entrepreneur. This should be experience gained in the early years. Their coaching or training must be on, or from, the job. The business has to carry on while our entrepreneur learns. Their self-development should be strategic.

The entrepreneur should read management books, and/or books on the economy. Wider learning from management tools such as these over time, become invaluable. The knowledge gained, even if they learn only one thing per book, enables the entrepreneur to grow. This growth develops over a period of time as they talk and engage with other professionals and entrepreneurs at events.

Other entrepreneurs are experiencing the same problems and issues. They can relate their own experiences and provide useful contacts to deal with problems and issues on recruitment, employment law, process and project management etc, as well as the latest excellent books to read.

The fountain of knowledge put down on paper by someone who has been there before is second to none, so to use and engage and receive that knowledge is testimony to the entrepreneur's own willingness to learn and ultimately to be successful.

They may themselves speak at these functions, becoming a relatively famous person themselves. All of these activities may take them out of their comfort zone, but they also broaden their horizons. Similar to their attendance on management courses, it develops the entrepreneur 'externally'.

There is no straightforward manual on selling or how to develop a team... a lot of it is intuition. There are management books and these are part of the toolbox, that is all. The entrepreneur will be able to do this as a result of their interpersonal skills mentioned above. Charisma and leadership should enable them to succeed in this area.

A further issue to consider would be the use of consultants.

Anyone who has had experience of consultants will realise that they come at a cost, as they are generally on a day rate, which seems exorbitant and, unless highly recommended, they seem to only tell you what you already know. The phrase 'no-one ever got fired for buying IBM' resonates with the experience of using consultants. However, they can be very useful as part of the make-up of a team to support the entrepreneur.

They are useful for providing the following:

- expertise in an area not already in-house,

- a separate and impassionate view,

- a resource when exceptional levels of work in the ordinary course of business occurs,

- an external resource when a piece of work needs to be fulfilled which is not in the ordinary course of business such as an acquisition or disposal,

- someone to blame for a decision,

- the support as an interim measure before a hire, or to justify a hire.

The consultant's brief must be clear, concise and deliverable on time, as well. The consultant will be charging premium rates and the entrepreneur will be under severe criticism from within, if the consultant does not perform.

However, there will not be criticism if the opposite applies and the entrepreneur creates an effective and highly talented board around him. The role of the board in any business is vital.

The board needs to include a chairperson, someone as a leading light in the industry or with good and relevant experience. This can be fulfilled by the entrepreneur and almost certainly will, unless they feel they can only take the business so far, and requires experience from, say, a non-executive chairman.

The non-executive will appear for board meetings and may take on a variety of roles within the organisation such as chairing meetings on:

- Planning and strategy

- If the business is large enough – executive remuneration

- The audit committee as corporate governance is critical for external relations

- Finance.

The rest of the board would generally be functional and the board member is directly responsible for the function, not only its smooth running but the direction and strategy within the overall business strategy. The board member must explore the activity within and measure it against the activity outside of the organisation. A well-balanced, suitably experienced and effective board aids and assists the entrepreneur to a large extent.

An entrepreneur may operate on their own at the start of the business and a non-executive chairman 'figure' can be extremely useful as a sounding board, say once or twice a year.

The entrepreneur should also seek such advice and guidance from professionals, also from external organisations who can support them. Organisations can provide this activity, virtual or franchised, however their competence and commitment must be tested and recommendations are essential.

Is the 'virtual' or 'alternative' board going to provide the support the entrepreneur seeks? The entrepreneur needs a team around them that is suitably experienced and will deliver the necessary drive and vision. There are many organisations providing a consultancy type of support at this level and care must be taken if they are to be engaged.

The structure and experience of the board is the key to success.

Any financier will back a business driver. Management is the key to a business's success.

The worst example of the construction of an executive board is the make-up of the government and the cabinet.

- **Prime Minister, First Lord of the Treasury and Minister for the Civil Service**

  (or the boss)

  - Deputy Prime Minister, Lord President of the Council
  - First Secretary of State, Secretary of State for Foreign and Commonwealth Affairs

- Chancellor of the Exchequer
- Chief Secretary to the Treasury
- Secretary of State for the Home Department
- Secretary of State for Defence
- Secretary of State for Business, Innovation and Skills; and President of the Board of Trade
- Secretary of State for Work and Pensions
- Lord Chancellor, Secretary of State for Justice
- Secretary of State for Education
- Secretary of State for Communities and Local Government
- Secretary of State for Health
- Secretary of State for Environment, Food and Rural Affairs
- Secretary of State for International Development
- Secretary of State for Scotland
- Secretary of State for Energy and Climate Change
- Secretary of State for Transport
- Secretary of State for Culture, Media and Sport; and Minister for Women and Equalities
- Secretary of State for Northern Ireland
- Secretary of State for Wales
- Leader of the House of Lords, Chancellor of the Duchy of Lancaster –

Those who also attend Cabinet

- Minister without Portfolio
- Leader of the House of Commons, Lord Privy Seal
- Chief Whip (Parliamentary Secretary to the Treasury)
- Minister for the Cabinet Office, Paymaster General
- Minister for Government Policy, Cabinet Office
- Minister of State at the Cabinet Office and the Department for Education
- Minister without Portfolio (and Co-Chairman of the Conservative Party)
- Senior Minister of State (Faith and Communities), Department for Communities and Local Government and the Foreign and Commonwealth Office

- Minister of State (Universities and Science), Department for Business, Innovation and Skills
- Attorney General *

*attends Cabinet when Ministerial responsibilities are on the agenda

Just think of restructuring this into an effective management team. There are 32 roles, and the way this is currently structured, it appears that the Prime minister has 31 direct reports! Even if the list of those who only attend cabinet meetings are considered to be the direct reports this list is then reduced to 21, and in most text books, it states that six direct reports is the maximum for best practice. Make your own judgement on the effectiveness of this structure.

More effective management and governance from our government would be achieved by giving the deputy prime minister a proper role, as outlined below:

- **Prime Minister, First Lord of the Treasury and Minister for the Civil Service (Chairman)**

- **First Secretary of State, Secretary of State for Foreign and Commonwealth Affairs**

  - Secretary of State for International Development
  - Secretary of State for Scotland
  - Secretary of State for Northern Ireland
  - Secretary of State for Wales
  - Secretary of State for Defence

- **Chancellor of the Exchequer**

  - Chief Secretary to the Treasury
  - Secretary of State for Business, Innovation and Skills; and President of the Board of Trade
  - Secretary of State for Work and Pensions
  - Minister for the Cabinet Office, paymaster general

- **Secretary of State for the Home Department**

  - Lord Chancellor, Secretary of State for Justice
  - Secretary of State for Communities and Local Government

- Leader of the House of Lords, Chancellor of the Duchy of Lancaster
- Leader of the House of Commons, Lord Privy Seal
- Senior Minister of State (Faith and Communities), Department for Communities and Local Government and the Foreign and Commonwealth Office

- **Deputy Prime Minister, Lord President of the Council (Chair of essential internal services)**

  - Secretary of State for Education
  - Secretary of State for Health
  - Secretary of State for Environment, Food and Rural Affairs
  - Secretary of State for Energy and Climate Change
  - Secretary of State for Transport
  - Secretary of State for Culture, Media and Sport; and Minister for Women and Equalities
  - Minister of State at the Cabinet Office and the Department for Education
  - Minister of State (Universities and Science), Department for Business, Innovation and Skills

Those who also attend Cabinet who do not seem to have proper jobs could be removed to ensure the smooth running of government business:

- **Minister without Portfolio (strategy and objective setting)**

  - Chief Whip (Parliamentary Secretary to the Treasury)
  - Minister for Government Policy, Cabinet Office
  - Minister without Portfolio (and Co-Chairman of the Conservative Party)
  - Attorney General*
    (external executive to make sure governance exists)

This gives the Prime Minister five direct reports and structure. Any thoughts are welcome. This must create a more dynamic environment.

The main seats of government such as Prime Minister, Foreign Secretary, Chancellor and Home Secretary have always been considered the top jobs. If so, treat them as such and have others reporting directly to them for the salient roles. This would mean turning the civil service in to a more streamlined organisation and the people in grey suits may find that difficult to take. That is what being an entrepreneur is about. Making the difficult decisions and using the correct and available resources at the right time, to do the right jobs.

A number of areas that should be addressed as new seats at the table are ministries for, say, **youth** or **technology**, but the civil service is not packed with the most entrepreneurial of types. This may not happen in the next government reshuffle so please do not hold your breath.

4.3 Management success

There has been significant volatility in prices since the 1970s. All currencies, stocks commodities and latterly property prices have fluctuated and been far from a one- way bet.

Since that date, there have been four distinct financial crises: a large number of banks in a number of countries have collapsed at the same time. Each of these crises was followed by a recession. Recessions can be considered good things, in as much as they:

- allow (precipitate) the weaker businesses to fail,

- remove excessive capacity from the market place

- allow those quick on their feet or adaptable to change, particularly these days in respect of technology, to succeed and take market advantage.

Again what is interesting about the past few financial crises is that they were preceded by credit bubbles. However this section is not about risk, which has been covered above. The purpose of mentioning recession here is to comment on one attribute rarely mentioned about entrepreneurs and not mentioned in this book so far, their almost 6th sense – vision.

If, in the UK, the 1970s crash was property-based, the late 1980s was manufacturing-based, and subsequent to that, the late 2000s was credit and property-based (again), then certain signals and data must be able to predict this turn of events. (The Asian crisis in the late 1990s did not hit the UK as hard as the other three.)

Equally an entrepreneur must 'get into' and understand their business.

Vision is required to see that there is a market. They must take each and every opportunity as it arrives and when the business peaks or they can offer little else, they must be ready to 'get out'.

The entrepreneur must have the foresight and critical thinking to get everything organised and correct, and most importantly, set up in the right order.

They have no satellite navigation to programme – just their intuition, so, as said before, they must possess a 6th sense. Their vision has to be 360-degree. All-round vision is required for the market, the production operation and the customers and the suppliers, not forgetting key, good, reliable employees.

Entrepreneurs do not understand those who do not possess this vision.

It is extremely frustrating and often taken as a vote of 'no confidence' and negativity by the entrepreneur on their cherished activity, strategy and plan. This is not demonstrated as clearly by those around him. The negativity will be shown as limited foresight and a failure to take risks by those associated with the entrepreneur. They support the entrepreneur but do not wish to be associated or perhaps blamed for any failure.

The other concept similar to vision, but not entirely aligned, is the entrepreneur's ability to change and adapt. An obvious example of an industry that has had to change and adapt over the century that perhaps was set in its ways is that of the retail grocery shops, soon to become 'supermarkets', then 'out of town outlets', now '24 hour local stores' and obviously 'online shopping' - providing deliveries direct to the consumer. At the time of writing it is well-known that one provider does not have this facility and is falling behind in terms of market share.

Management techniques to identify the business's opportunities are long in the tooth, with the favourite being:

Strengths	Weaknesses
Opportunities	Threats

This relates to the business and not the entrepreneur. This is important as it can easily identify where attention and action is needed.

However the best diagram to see how successful the entrepreneur will be is set out below.

Every entrepreneur (and employee) wants to do the right thing right, this is pretty obvious. To do so, they must be adequately equipped and trained.

No entrepreneur or employee wishes to do the wrong thing wrong. To do so, will mean a short business life. So let's discuss the boxes in bold.

Right Thing Right	**Right Thing Wrong**
Wrong Thing Right	Wrong Thing Wrong

The entrepreneur can from time to time have employees do the right thing, but wrong. This is could considered to be relatively good news as it is effectively the employee doing the right thing but the employee just needs training to do it correctly. In accounting terms it could be, as an example, the monthly bank reconciliation which is completed every month – the right thing, but never balanced – the wrong thing. Training is easily available to correct this.

Therefore, simple training and practice is required for the employee to perform this activity correctly. Again moving on, the entrepreneur probably knows it is done each month but not agreed, and does not provide the employee with the training. The right activity is performed but is done incorrectly. The correct step would be to provide the training and management supervision. This is example is not life threatening to the business. Others could be.

The wrong thing right is strategic. Almost every entrepreneur in a start-up business will be doing the wrong thing in a number of their activities, but of course, doing it right. This can be as simple as putting stamps on envelopes before he has secretarial support. Of course, this should not really be the chief executive's, role but needs must. It is done correctly as every letter finds its way to its destination.

Perhaps a more meaningful example would be scheduling the chief executive's own diary for business prospects (given certain parameters for the target customers). This activity can be done by another person less skilled. Quantifying the lead and organising the schedule is not an activity that the chief executive should do, they are better attending the meetings, advising and winning the valuable business from the client.

So, in another example, it is a strategic move to understand that the entrepreneur needs to hire a market research person, in house or as a consultant. The activity is correct but need not be performed by the chief executive. The wrong thing is being carried out by the entrepreneur, but they are doing it correctly. As a result they then find they have a busy diary and have won even more contracts and the firm has become even more successful.

Whatever stage the entrepreneur is at in their business life cycle they will still carry out the 'wrong thing right' for some activities for a while.

Clever entrepreneurs will do these activities during downtime or even quietly and secretly as there is comfort in doing some simple or routine tasks. Reviewing the production schedule in detail or analysing some 'what ifs' in the cash flow, are not their job but useful exercises, still.

The shrewd employees wishing to get on and also more importantly empathise with the entrepreneur will assist them by taking these activities away from them. Doing them and performing them well, but allowing the bigger picture to function extremely well as a result by allowing the entrepreneur to do – the right thing right.

£££ OUR SURVEY ASKED

Is there another skill required for the successful entrepreneur?

Free-format answers were:

- Having a great team around you
- Product and market knowledge
- Ability to recognise and execute a market opportunity
- Adaptability
- Balancing all the skills required
- People management and motivation

All very subjective, but they do demonstrate the charisma and vision required as well as the ability to manage people and situations, and adapt.

A number of would-be entrepreneurs would like to get to the end game quickly, build the business, show the trappings of success and sell. They would therefore be selling an intangible asset, such as the future goodwill of the business, which is a difficult yet not impossible dream. Their charisma will be called upon in this situation.

The business would be flawed if it was missing a vital ingredient. This would (could?) take the form of a key senior employee. It may also be too much reliance on one customer or supplier. However, to the right buyer this could also be a definite attraction. It may make the business cheaper on sale and therefore, while this is covered in the section 'Trade-in, it is tantamount to the smooth acceleration of the business and the entrepreneur taking '100 little steps'.

'100 little steps' means taking time over growth and strategy, taking matters in an orderly fashion, in a timely and considered basis and growing a sustainable business.

The often-used phrase 'Rome was not built in a day' is extremely relevant to the entrepreneur. This manifests itself when the entrepreneur considers the strategy and growth of his business, not extending themselves with their resources.

Cash resource is the obvious one when considering growth, but for the entrepreneur their own 'time' is always at a premium and hence the critical discussion on the tools mentioned above. Doing the right thing right all the while through the '100 little steps' will build a worthwhile and highly sustainable business.

The 100 little steps can be broken down into five to 10 sections or mini milestones. At each stage on the milestone, a mini strategic review of the business can be taken.

£££ OUR SURVEY ASKED
Have you set yourself identifiable milestones to achieve?
52% answered yes

This is a low statistic for forward-looking successful entrepreneurs and shows a lack of attention to the numbers.

£££ OUR SURVEY ASKED
If yes, and if you have achieved that first milestone, did you immediately present yourself with another milestone?
40% of the 52% above answered yes

Perhaps a full strategic review should be undertaken after two years from the start of the business or the first draft of the setting of the initial strategy and the 100 little steps, and then again after say 40 of those little steps.

The 100th step is to sell, or groom the business for sale.

It should not be considered easy to set the steps, and it may be that only four visionary milestones can be set. The first major milestone may be at step 15 and therefore there are 15 smaller steps to get there. Without achieving these, you will not get to the first major milestone.

This is not literal, in as much as we need 100 individual identifiers, but 10 mini milestones as part of the 100 may look something like this:

- launch product 1 or branch 1 (15)

- ensure finance in place for development of product 3 or branch 3 (10)

- obtain 25th customer spending over £ (5)

- open further production facility (15)

- engage full time sales director (15)

- achieve £x million of sales (10)

- engage non-executive (industry known) chairman (5)

- achieve £y million of sales (5)

- sustain profits and pay off loans (10)

- attract suitors to the business and groom for sale (10)

When these have been identified and agreed, the functions required to deliver each will become obvious. This breaks the milestones down into small functions enabling the milestones to be achieved easily.

Any batsman building an innings would be looking to bat in 15- or 30-minute chunks, staying at the crease and building an innings, not getting out. As a direct result of this runs for the team (perhaps considered the primary objective) are scored. 'Runs will come.'

When the business is reaching the 4th or even 5th milestone, a further review of its overall objectives and resources, especially manpower and their abilities to take it to the next stage, would be useful. The initial direction of the business may have changed and a total review very necessary. A review of the team, can the team deliver the next phase? Are the key people in the right positions?

As a football team moves up the various leagues, the players undoubtedly change. A conference league player is not necessarily as skilled or as physically fit as a premier league player, otherwise, surely they would playing in the premier league.

Attention must be given to the overall strategy while attending to details. This vision must not be overlooked and cannot necessarily be delegated by the entrepreneur. Their attention to strategy, vision and implementation makes them what they are.

Their ability to dip into the detail is not a negative. Employees must empathise that that gives the entrepreneur comfort that what they are building is sustainable and valuable. The entrepreneur needs the team to complete the detail.

4.4 Reading the key performance indicators

Management information is the vitality of any organisation.

If the entrepreneur does not know how they are doing across both the financial and non-financial performance of the company then it is hardly worth getting out of bed to go to work, to monitor the excellent performance or even to improve less than satisfactory performance.

Hence the need to prepare forecasts and the need to understand the profit and loss account, particularly the difference between gross profit and net profit. There is also a need to control overheads, create and manage the balance sheet and establish cash flow. Most importantly non-financial measures can lead to better financial performance and act as indicators for the future which the entrepreneur can read and understand to help their vision.

£££ OUR SURVEY ASKED

What are your first three milestones?

	Rank out 3
A profit figure	1.72
To earn a living	1.20
A sales figure	1.04
To increase your net wealth	0.92
To prove you could do it to yourself	0.60
To repay seed capital	0.28
To prove you could do it to others	0.20

Considering that these were marked 1, 2 and 3 to score on average around 2, then our entrepreneurs were very realistic that profit and earning a living were key to success.

This is not a text book on finance for the non-financial manager, but reading and understanding such a book can only stand the entrepreneur in good stead. This will also allow them to focus on key performance indicators (often referred to as KPI's). One critical KPI would be the daily sales or takings for the business, perhaps per outlet or by product.

Q. What is wrong with this level of minutiae?

A. Absolutely nothing.

To understand the need for data, however detailed, or wherever it may be in the organisation, shows an element of control, responsibility and understanding in respect of what constituent parts make the business tick.

The profit and loss account is critical to the business. The business has to make a profit, the profit generates assets and our 15th-century Franciscan Friar, Luca Pacioli has a lot to answer for and deserves a lot of credit (profit), which generates an asset (debit).

Pacioli decided that every entry had to be entered twice, a debit deserves a credit and therefore that 'equity = assets less liabilities'. For those in the know (qualified accountants) this is simplicity in the extreme and does mean that accountants can often talk in a foreign language – particularly to our entrepreneur. The entrepreneur may not be trained in accounting or business management and needs the results described in simple yet clear terms with perhaps graphs and diagrams. Yet a basic understanding of accounting could be considered not only fundamental but also an advantage to the entrepreneur.

Italians such Amatino Manucci a Florentine merchant from the late 13th century, Farolfi and Co, a firm of merchants in Florence acting as money lenders, and also early records of the Medici bank in the 14th century, showed evidence of double entry bookkeeping in their ledgers. Here ends the history lesson. The Republic of Genoa has accounts demonstrating this method but our friend Pacioli codified the system.

The profit and loss account is simply a trading statement on an accruals basis. This means 'not based on cash received and paid basis' and determines the profit (or loss) generated by the business over a given period, taking in to account amounts receivable and payable in the future.

The two important figures from this statement are the gross and net profit.

The gross profit means the amount that any organisation generates as a contribution to sales. You can sell 1000 widgets for £2000 and make £1000 or you can sell 1000 gadgets at £2000, with your sales at the top line showing the same finite figure and make £500. Which do you prefer to sell? Which makes the higher gross profit? Obviously the widgets, as the cost of sales is less, being £1000 compared to £1500. You owe the supplier less and as long as the sale of widgets maintains this level, this is the better business model.

The gross profit or contribution by service, type, product, outlet, area, a period of time (adjusting for seasons) country or production facility is important. At this level we can quickly identify faults with sales lines, outlets, production facilities etc. It is a highly measurable and performance-linked figure. Businesses with low gross profit margins have to work so much harder to achieve success. High gross profit margins are attractive businesses for any investor.

The information provided must be timely and accurate to be valuable.

This management information should be shown simply and in the form of non-financial schedules for the entrepreneur, perhaps with headline figures and % on one page. It is always useful to mark what the plan or forecast was set at. Our widgets above are outperforming the forecast, as we thought we would sell 800 at a gross profit of £600, so we are better not only with the number sold but also its contribution, why?

Many entrepreneurs will not trust the forecast but if they have (quite rightly) signed off on the forecast or budget as 'do-able' and realistic, then the performance at the factory (a good quality product) the sales team (generating the sales) and the marketing team (creating awareness at the right price) all need to be commended.

The interpretation of performance and variance analysis is as critical as the production of the numbers.

The forecasts and trading statements are not just for good news but also for bad news. It is clear that the performance of the gadgets may not be to forecast and questions may need answering. The questions to be posed are the results from the figures obtained. Is the product quality in question, is the sales team concentrating on a product where they can easily earn commission, or is the market awareness simply not there, and the price wrong?

All of these questions can only be answered by considered thought and reviewing trends.

The entrepreneur needs this management information, boiled down to easy-to-understand constituent parts. They should not be asking the questions nor at the very least asking for the information. It should be provided as a matter of course.

This profit and loss statement also needs the overhead figures, as that turns the gross profit into a net profit.

£££ OUR SURVEY ASKED

Do you have key performance indicators in your business?

	% answered by rank
Monthly	76%
Weekly	41%
Daily	29%
One important one	27%
Never	4%

Obviously some entrepreneurs answered with one or more answers but an extremely high percentage, 41% said weekly. It could be argued this should be 100% to exercise control and to know what is happening. Daily can be considered overkill, but many do, 29% – nearly a third! **To see 76% answered monthly is comforting.**

As mentioned above, a source of finance is managing the company's assets efficiently, and therefore we need to review the effect of the balance sheet.

Taking each category of asset in the balance sheet separately, hopefully they can be easily understood.

Fixed assets need to be acquired as efficiently as possible. Possibly over the length of their life and also a policy on reinvestment must be followed religiously to ensure that they are working efficiently. A policy on reinvestment should be followed religiously, possibly over the full length of the assets' life, to ensure they are individually within the total plant working efficiently. Efficient working of the plant and equipment means that repairs, faulty goods, management time and general all-round inefficiencies can be kept to a minimum.

Running a production facility would mean that hours in production or more importantly hours 'out of production' for the plant would be a very important statistic. This is a **KPI** of prime importance for the production director and entrepreneur. Should the plant be upgraded, will there be an expensive repair or will the downtime mean a lack of product resulting in a lack of sales and a loss?

An investment from the business in another venture or a loan, should only be done with excess cash on hand and possibly [only] if the investment is to pay dividends in the meantime. A very good reason may be to set up another entrepreneur in a business alongside. This may be a would-be supplier or an add-on or affiliated service, perhaps.

Research and development fits in to this category, if it is worthy of being capitalised and not incurred as expenditure in the accounting period. It should be placed on the balance sheet if it is realisable.

The thorny subject of work-in-progress and stock-holding comes next.

Many entrepreneurs and perhaps even finance professionals do not realise the 'play' to be had in these numbers, work-in-progress or stockholding, alone. It is very surprising that the tax and revenue officials do not ask for a detailed analysis of this figure as a matter of course. This is where profits are made or lost – and worse still, hidden or deferred.

Work-in-progress is exactly that. It relates to items which have been incurred by the business but not yet realised. This is ordinarily seen in a business with long-term projects.

Work in progress can easily be explained as the cost of a construction contract (or part thereof) for which no sale is recognised in the relevant accounting period. It is an asset the business has on the balance sheet at cost. The higher the value of work-in-progress means the more cost that is deferred in the relevant past period. This results in more profit being recognised in the relevant period which is being reported.

Again the corollary would be to be able to write off the work-in-progress, then the sales which are yet to be recognised for the business to make a future profit in the following periods. The value of work-in-progress can be recognised in days, such as stock turn.

Stock holding must be reviewed regularly. Is the business holding old or slow-moving stock? Both of these would make the value of the stock unrealisable at the levels shown on the balance sheet.

Accounts receivable are another asset regularly referred to as 'debtors'. These must be regularly reviewed and the review is to ensure that the business is not chasing debts that are non-collectable, are there specific reasons for non-payment? The customers may be holding up payment of thousands of pounds for a £10 credit note. This is not a very fair-minded customer, but the problem is perhaps about poor internal control rather than the customer's issue.

These assets should be given priority and measured with relevance to each individual business, but ordinarily, the lower they are, then the less finance is required.

The finance is on the other side of the balance sheet, perhaps a bank overdraft, loans, trade creditors, government taxes or even retained equity.

The debtor days and stock turn days are easily calculated by using the following equation for any given period:

Debtor days:

Sales for the period, adding any sales tax (if relevant) divided by the days in the period, giving an average sale per day.

Taking the outstanding debtors and dividing this by the sales per day provides the answer to the above equation.

Unless you are a cash business, under 30 days is very good. 40-60 days is average and over 60 days or two months on average to collect your debt is poor. This very statistic or **KPI** can put the best and most profitable businesses out of business. This is nothing new, but is frequently not understood and frequently overlooked, until it is too late.

'They are a good customer, don't chase too hard.' This statement is tantamount to weak management.

An example:

Sales for the 6 months are £750,000

Debtors on the balance sheet are £222,000

What are the debtor days?

£750,000 * 1.2 (to include VAT) * 2 for an annual figure divided by 365 gives a value of sales per day = £4,931

£222,000 divided by £4,931 = 45 days, or a month and a half. Good!

Stock turn:

Cost (purchases) of sales for the period, not adding any sales tax, divided by the days in the period, giving an average cost or amount purchased per day.

Taking the value of stock (include sales tax if not already included) and dividing this by the cost or amount purchased per day, provides the answer to the above equation.

This gives you the average amount of time that stock is held, known as stock turn. If this is a business where the stock has a distinct shelf life such as food, then surely this should be very low, possibly under seven days. The KPI is particularly useful for ranges of stock as then the slow-moving items can be identified. They surely have no or little value and should not be held at cost. Writing off of this type of stock reduces profitability.

Many businesses stock to order and, during a recession, customers may notice that their orders are slower to turn around, rather than quicker to turn around. Instead of being taken from a surplus of stock waiting to be sold, it is quite the opposite. A slower turn around would be the mark of a good, well-managed organisation fulfilling orders as they are given and committed to by payment. Only at this point does the business offer the complete range of product by size and colour, without having it ready-made on the off-chance you may appear with your cheque book. Give the business time, be patient and realise that they intend to be there to service and maintain your custom in the future.

This demonstrates the savvy and careful entrepreneur.

An example:

Cost of sales for the year is £1,250,000

Stock on the balance sheet is £475,000

What is the stock turn?

£1,250,000 divided by 365 gives a value of cost of sales per day = £3,424

£475,000 divided by £3,424 = 138 days, or 4.5 months. Slow turn, poor?

The last key piece of management information, and possibly the most critical to survival, would be the cash flow of the business. This demonstrates how the profit generates cash and how it is spent, and in some respects this is the most important piece of financial information.

The question many financiers and backers will ask is, is the business generating cash and if not, why not?

Most financiers looking at businesses as prospects request this information and it can only be respected if it relates accurately or ties back to the profit and loss account, for example, if it can be reconciled to profits and the balance sheet for the same periods.

It will be in a different format to the profit and loss account. It will show spikes of cash required generally for employee costs and government taxes as they fall due and then as cash comes into the business, the cash will be positive.

This schedule will show the cash requirement of the business. If the cash requirement is more than anyone is prepared to borrow then the business could well become insolvent and unable to trade.

The cash flow is summarised in statutory accounts in the source and application of funds statement. This perhaps is the most critical statement in any reporting and could be said to be essential to any form of management reporting.

The source of funds is the profit stated on a cash basis. The application of funds will be the opposite of that – it would show allocation of funds, such as asset purchases, say. This amount generated is itself reconciled back to the increase or decrease in working capital, looking at how receivables, payables and loans may have moved.

How many times do entrepreneurs think they make a profit but cannot understand why there is no money is the bank? Who has spent it? No-one has – it has just gone into increased 'debtor days' or 'slow-moving stock' as shown above and worse still into 'work in progress' which will not be realised for some time until it is invoiced. Therefore the bank may be reluctant to fund further monies, apparently thereby losing patience and unable to extend finance.

The KPIs mentioned are some highlights amongst many.

This leads us nicely to non-financial statistics or KPIs. Receiving management information is not just about reporting on financial results or forecasts. Of course this is fundamental to the profitability but early warning signals and/or the resulting profit can be read and forecast from statistics or KPI's of a non-financial nature.

To understand that the sales force, team or those responsible for sales are making calls, arranging meetings, seeing customers, making quotes, can only lead to the generation of sales.

Statistics demonstrating each salesperson's activity would be a leading KPI for an organisation which is sales driven or order lead. It may be that a sales person should be set three or four meetings a day, 20 a week, or 80 in a month. That requires careful planning and organisation and is a very steep task.

It may be best to reduce it to allow for preparation, quality of calls, time taken at each meeting and also to prevent burn out. The finite number is a monitor and one from which activity can be evaluated – but the sales person with the most fertile patch need make one call or meeting and deliver the same in terms of orders than another working to the extremes of their patch and making 80 calls. Reality needs to kick in to the finite measurement.

Just to target activity as one number is as weak a metric measure of the success of our sales person working for the entrepreneur as the single academic level of 51% achieved in an examination in the section on measuring intelligence.

So to quantify and measure the meetings with new customers and existing customers would be a much better target. Perhaps this could take the form of establishing how many customers a salesperson should have as a portfolio. If they currently have 240 then to schedule annual maintenance calls there should be one made for each customer once a year which is (with four weeks' holiday) five a week or one day. This is a very reasonable target and schedule, indeed.

Alternatively, we can presume that we can give the salesperson leads and that they should be able to manage 15 meetings a week, as long as travel allows. Then around seven to 10 new client meetings a week is a reasonable activity to measure. If this is achieved then the salesperson is doing the right thing right. If the salesperson is not converting those leads into new customers at say a recognised ratio of 2 per week, another question can be brought in to play. Are they any good, do they say the right thing, is the quality of lead any good? Across 10 sales people mean averages of performance can be calculated over a period of time. This is all good management information to refine and interpret and use as measurement of an expected level of performance and to adjust where necessary and to judge the 'expected activity'.

Another piece of non-financial information to interpret may be the number of estimates produced by the estimating department for potential orders. This can be related to the number won. If over a month, say, the experience is 30%, or three orders in 10 estimates, then the entrepreneur can judge what the business should expect and guidelines can be laid down. Say the business has a turnover of £1.8m per annum of £150,000 per month, made up of 10 activities on average at between £5,000 and £25,000 per sale, then any work on an estimate over £50,000, while nice to have, would put undue pressure on the business operations to fulfil it.

If the estimating department got a job in at say a value of £300,000, then it would be nonsensical to estimate this job and to spend time trying to work out its total value and constituent costs for the end customer, as it would not be possible, unless it was sub-contracted out, to be able to produce it through the current production facility. The order may relate to ready-made parts and therefore may be possible to fulfil. All of these issues can be built into KPIs or empirical data to manage that area and important function of the business.

If the success rate drops below the expected norm of 30%, then there could be a number of factors to consider:

- The industry pricing has shifted due to excess capacity, competitors are under cutting

- We are building in prices rises on materials or labour that need to be absorbed

- Our profit margins are too high

- The quality of leads are poor and we are not making the correct mark in to the market of 'our' jobs between £5,000 and £25,000

- The estimates are not produced on a timely basis

- The quality of work has been poor.

This is the lifeline of the company and needs careful review and monitoring as the leads and estimates drying up will have a direct correlation to the sales and lack of contribution to overhead, resulting in losses.

Adequate management information for the entrepreneur on this area will help them understand the forward business.

Another example of using information may be the empirical data or KPI for the pipeline of business. For example, this can be produced within a small-town commercial property agency when property is launched and to judge or evaluate the market reaction. Data can be accumulated, such as enquiries within five days, six to 14 days and days thereafter, and from this it can be ascertained what further marketing needs to be undertaken. Or equally any alteration to the property details itself, as surely the first few enquiries will sort out its inadequacies etc. Data on any subject can produce a varying degree of interpretation and lead to success. In this example, the key would be to shorten the length of time between marketing a property and either selling or letting it.

Agency commission derived is how this property agent will be remunerated and will be how their reputation is enhanced or not. Do they move the property along? As boring as the collection of the data may be, the lateral thought, in this respect, improves activity if it is interpreted and acted upon. This example proves that data and statistics can be drawn from many different sources across all activities.

The entrepreneur must understand this and not allow it to cloud their judgement and improve their ego. One 'dashboard' with, say, 'five key numbers' and even daily flash figures to keep the entrepreneur up to date are extremely suitable for allowing them to manage their business with the utmost control.

The successful entrepreneur is one who sets realistic targets, expects and reads their KPI's dutifully. Thereby controlling the organisations they have created.

They read and understand their dashboards.

CHAPTER FIVE

GOING UP THE GEARS

5.1 Introduction

To set the scene for this chapter the entrepreneur now runs a business with staff. The entrepreneur has to use their skills and character to get the best out of those around them to develop the business. They cannot, and are delusionary if they think they can, do it all themselves. They need:

- A team

- To create a culture

- To develop the products or intellectual property

- To put in place a sales team

- The result of all of these will lead to a defined strategy and a business not centred on the entrepreneur themselves.

Without thinking ahead and creating a strategy they will make their business merely a job – perhaps a better job than working for someone else, but with more risk. The job will not bear the fruits and rewards they think it should, but a well-managed business and strategy will produce such fruit. It is by developing the team around the entrepreneur that the business will develop the best outcome, by far.

We investigate the entrepreneur's ability to develop a strategy and vision not only to grow their own skills but also that of the team.

The entrepreneur, with the ability to empathise and communicate those visions to the team will be the one who succeeds.

5.2 Team development and understanding others

Once the entrepreneur has alighted upon their idea and the business develops, the strengths and weaknesses of their personality will come to the fore very quickly. As soon as anything develops in the business it changes the dynamics and the metamorphosis of the business creates its own issues.

Developing a team around themselves is a lot easier said than put into effect. One of the key areas that the entrepreneur has to realise is that they cannot put everything into effect alone. Key appointments need and have to be made.

While the business is trading at a relatively sound pace and growing year on year in terms of sales and profits, the staff affecting this development are the employees and not necessarily the business drivers. This is because the business effectively is propelling itself forward. The employees may be taking instructions from the entrepreneur and not questioning their reason. They will be following orders not thinking of the consequences nor the risk and rewards to be gained through these orders. The employees are simply doing their jobs to the best of their ability and they are hopefully creating a business renowned for its product service and delivery, and for positioning the pricing well. The employees will be blissfully unaware of the intricacies of the balance sheet, both good or bad.

OUR SURVEY ASKED...

Do you recognise any weaknesses in yourself?
96% said yes

Have you compensated for those weaknesses?
72% said yes

This is a set of statistics from a very well-rounded group of people, well aware of their own limitations. These are not statistics from a set of pig headed, arrogant or bombastic set of people.

On the other hand, a business driver will be looking to develop the business and to do so they need confidence. Therefore, they will be evaluating the decisions in terms of risk and reward. The business driver should be the entrepreneur themselves but it is not necessarily the case.

The business driver may be another Director and perhaps take the form of a non-executive Director. The role may even be a President or a Chairperson.

A business driver is someone who either has the ability to change strategy or introduce an outside concept or idea or process into the business to improve it.

The chairperson in this instance, not actually being the entrepreneur, is a very important person in the organisation. They almost certainly will be the voice of:

- Measurement

- Calm

- Industry experience

- Industry contacts

(When you watch the old Westerns with John Wayne or Jimmy Stewart, the Indian tribes generally have a sage or an old, wise chief. From this picture the non-executive Chairperson is born.)

However, having stated that this role is of paramount importance it can only exist, and more importantly critically succeed, if the entrepreneur respects and listens to the words of wisdom and guidance offered by the person in this position. It can become a critical position if used properly.

The entrepreneur has to trust this person. Their relationship with the chairperson has to be fair, or the whole business could be in jeopardy, principally because the breakdown will lead to factional decision-making. The strength of the board is the key to the development of the strategy – the ability of the board to set far reaching and far thinking plans. The board must act as one. The entrepreneur cannot undermine the chairperson.

Outsiders will respect the constituency of the board and, of course, not only will the business gain respect in its own industry but also one of the key outcomes will be the ability to attract other good and experienced personnel. Increased credibility will have a far-reaching affect, including increasing the business's ability to borrow and develop.

The team gives it credibility and a track record, particularly if one or any of the new members have developed businesses and raised venture capital or borrowed funds before. Their attitude and responsibility to borrowing and the borrower goes a long way to the business being able to furnish a well thought-out business plan, justifying the borrowing requirement and the lender being happy to provide the funds.

The trust involved within and outside the organisation by this key appointment manifests itself in its success at:

- The raising of finance

- Its ability to recruit key players within the industry

- Its profile

- Its standing in the industry

- Its trust measurement

The measurement of trust can be sampled in a simple document. The first section must be to measure your own trust, and that means the entrepreneur's own internal trust. How they measure themselves? Do their actions and words match congruently? Do they speak the truth all the time? Do they carry out what they say they will?

This establishes the entrepreneur's own credibility and integrity. If this is in doubt then they have no hope in being able to instill this in others and of course, expect it from others.

The entrepreneur must demonstrate trust in those around them, particularly those close to them and the trust must be to take the rough with the smooth to understand that while others may not have as much at risk, they do care, they will care about the job and their performance, and the test is for the entrepreneur to enable them to feel very wanted within the organisation.

Much is written in management books about the art or science of management but unless the entrepreneur can develop techniques to goad the team to perform, there is not much hope. The entrepreneur must be trusted by others, which is generally achieved by regular and consistent performance. This is also demonstrated by their passion and energy. This is true with the relationship between the entrepreneur and the appointed chairperson. It must be seen to work.

With the appointment of a non-executive or a chairperson then it is even more important to put in place an effective chain of command. This has to exist, as there are clearly two important people at the helm of the organisation – not one – once a non-executive chairperson is involved.

Who do the employees take their instructions from?

Equally these may not be the only two, and there could be more board members. It is not for this section, but of course the constituency of any board needs to be made of the 'super' heads of departments or functions. This can be simply put as being the head of sales, production, accounts, operations and marketing.

However, as we saw with the example of the structure of the government, the heads of certain functions closely aligned to various board functions can report into those board members. It really depends on what works and what fits for each organisation. There has to be representation on the board for every function. There may be a good reason to have a board member for 'customer delivery' as well as for 'new customers', alongside operations and of course conflict is healthy as long as it is fair, measured and 'chaired'. In presiding over such conflicts this may become a key role of the new non-executive chairperson, and/or their resolution. It would be inappropriate if the non-executive chairperson and entrepreneur's sole roles were that of arbitrators.

The entrepreneur or chairperson in this instance has to be totally non-judgemental and not favour certain founding employees, customers or employees. As soon as the board develops to act in unison or seen to be a 'band of brothers', it becomes obvious that history has moved on and the business is not the entrepreneur's. It is ageing and maturing. This will be faced much more unequivocally when the entrepreneur considers selling, as seen in the section, entitled 'the trade in' but for now the entrepreneur is learning. They are learning to trust their judgement with appointments. This is a difficult first move but the way they approach this is fundamental to the next steps of their and their business's development.

The function of the non-executive chairperson, as we have called it here, must have clear objectives on strategy set by the entrepreneur and chairperson themselves. These must be clearly communicated to the board. If these are not communicated then the board members will quickly fall out with the concept.

This is dealt with in the last piece of this section.

As we saw before, 40% of our entrepreneurs decided to employ a chairperson with only 20% (or half of the 40%) actually doing so.

The entrepreneur does not have to over-egg his explanation of the role of the non-executive chairperson, but it can easily be explained as filling the gap or gaps that the entrepreneurs cannot fill themselves.

The entrepreneur must tell those around them exactly where they are deficient. It may be simply management techniques. As the entrepreneur may not be able to implement procedures and a clearly defined management information structure of reports and deliverables, let alone monitor their functionality and that of other directors, employees and staff to meet the necessary criteria.

Often entrepreneurs become disappointed and disillusioned by a lack of ability and drive from employees and even senior employees unable to complete projects.

This disappointment manifests itself in the entrepreneur taking on yet more functions themselves and not delegating as much as they should. Key employees are as much to blame for this as the entrepreneur. They should step up to the mark and realise how much the entrepreneur has on their plate. Staff must align themselves with the entrepreneur and hopefully prove they are worthy of promotion and more responsibility. They must place their trust in the entrepreneur and match the entrepreneur. The entrepreneur is a doer and achiever/completer by their very nature.

Incentivising staff can be best achieved with a bonus or share scheme. This unfortunately comes down to the original motivating force for the entrepreneur – money, as we have mentioned before.

Overall, the entrepreneur has a lonely job, often they will be at the helm of the business with no-one to turn to in respect of wide-ranging decisions. The entrepreneur will almost certainly take or make decisions – as we have seen above, they are a risk-taker in as much as they trust their own judgement, albeit not a risk defined as 'exposure to the possibility of loss, injury or other adverse or unwelcome circumstance.' But the assessment of a situation where there may be perceived risk needs to be reduced as much as possible.

Hence the need and comfort of having someone that they can bounce ideas off and discuss necessary changes, hires, developments or expenditure. The non-executive chairperson can be considered the 'voice of calm'. This is the 'voice of reason', and someone that the entrepreneur can respect and listen to. Therefore as discussed above the relationship between these two protagonists is essential to the well-being of the business.

The entrepreneur and the non-executive chairperson are allowed to disagree, this relationship may not always have 100% consensus. In that respect there has to be a maturity between them to sit down and openly discuss the best way forward. This should not lead to a parting of the ways but hopefully an agreement in the end and a stronger relationship.

If there is a fundamental disagreement, one where neither party can see themselves continuing as a result of the decision made, or rather not made, then yes, the two should part. This does not mean that either is wrong. Time will tell, as either the business will go on to achieve greater success or it will face its demise. As it would normally be the non-executive chairperson who departs, unless they wish to carry out a management buy-in, the entrepreneur will be left with the consequences of their actions. After all, the business remains the property of the entrepreneur.

The departure of the non-executive chairperson would be a great shame and generally a backward step for the business, as their appointment is a tremendous fillip to the business and one which should help project it forward. The non-executive may just not be the right person and the role itself should not be dismissed.

It would be interesting to analyse which decisions the two disagree on and are the differences so fundamental that they part ways. However, short discussions and disagreements should be dealt with appropriately such that they become and develop into agreement as quickly as possible. Any disagreement, however trivial, can be time-consuming and exhausting and take the focus away from the main game which is to develop the business. At this point the business is bigger than both of them.

The two should have worked in harmony and it is hoped they will have developed their well-honed and achievable strategy at the outset. This would of course, alleviate the need or possibility of argument, disagreement and facilitate harmony.

The entrepreneur will generally be quite inward looking. This is not a negative but something that often occurs by the very nature of the entrepreneur being a developer of their own business. The entrepreneurs who go to industry seminars, marketing conferences or exhibitions, will be aware of what is around them. However, that expertise itself does not match the experience of someone who has been in the industry for some years and knows its development and hopefully has a vision of its future. The non-executive chairperson will have the vision and judgement to be able to measure the direction of the business and assist the entrepreneur with that very same direction and most importantly passion.

If the right person is appointed, it can result in a truly enriching experience and lead to great success.

The entrepreneur (and the business) will actually benefit by having a sounding board within the organisation, in whatever form that may be.

The entrepreneur may seek other skills.

£££ OUR SURVEY ASKED...
Is there a skill base missing within your business, if so would you or have you recruited to fill that skill base?

	% saying yes
Marketing	53%
Selling	47%
Wider industry knowledge	33%
Operations	31%
Finance	29%
Research and development, inventiveness	27%

Our survey also asked whether the entrepreneur covered everything and 36% answered yes to the question!

While the entrepreneur obviously knows their product or service levels and is technically proficient within the industry, to have someone on board who has been in the industry longer or who is well-known within it, or even has been previously been successful is a great tangible benefit to the business. The industry knowledge and perhaps even dealings with the same customers is beneficial, as it is useful to have experience of problems or issues prior to them arising rather than as they arise. This way, any problems can be avoided or their impact reduced.

The knowledge gained will also be about competitors, such that the specialist talent held by the competitors can be monitored and possibly brought on board. Going from ordinary to better is about the processes in place, not necessarily the people who carry out the processes. Key production and sales people are worth having to become a yet better organisation and perhaps an industry leader.

These are all building blocks used by the entrepreneur to develop their team. All the while they must be mindful that they encourage, praise and coach the team. The entrepreneur is, obviously, the biggest winner but the team can give them the tools to carry out their dream.

The team can be incentivised. To do so, the entrepreneur's instructions must be clear and unequivocal, the objectives measurable and attainable.

The passion imparted by the entrepreneur and their drive and enthusiasm must be unwavering. This way the team will empathise with the entrepreneur and their ego and to trust them.

The number two within the organisation may be seeking to step up to the mark of the entrepreneur and take over. But, unless they have the skills, vision and abilities referred to here then they may not take the business to the next level. A difficult decision to make and it would be unfair to appoint and let them fail. Perhaps appointing them in to a minor role, yet with leadership requirements, as a starter to see them develop is a way forward and fair. Proof will be evident quickly if the deputy can deputise long term. (They didn't always succeed in those Westerns.)

The team is critical. The successful entrepreneur fully understands that requirement.

5.3 Legendary service and dealing with clients

Applying the latest technology enables the entrepreneur to keep up to date and at least stand a chance of providing legendary service to customers.

The innovations, now, should include:

- Document management systems

- Electronic processing and workflows

- Multiple monitors

- Portals

- Cloud computing

- CRM software

- iPad and iPhone communications

- 'Apps'

- Instant messaging and updates on stock, meetings, orders etc

Service is being renamed 'legendary service', as it creates the idea that it is about more than just ensuring the customer is satisfied. By renaming the term 'service' to be 'legendary service', the action should focus the team on who is important in the organisation. The entrepreneur needs to create the culture that not only is customer the 'paying master' but the unelected 'king' of the organisation.

Legendary service is the vernacular used to ensure that all team members remember how they should approach even a phone call from a customer or client. The call must take priority and time taken out to service the client or customer is very well spent.

Not many organisations focus on what the customer needs, they tend to focus on what they can offer the customer.

An excellent tool to establish this is set out below. Many organisations believe in old- fashioned customer surveys, but they only target the questions that they believe should be answered, rather than establishing the clients' needs and values. It is critical to establish what the customers' value. This is where the entrepreneur probably has a sixth sense. But they also need empirical evidence to test this out. Justification of results is a good thing.

First list the attributes of a business. These may be:

- Speed of delivery

- Pricing policies

- Range of products

- Showroom

- Website

- Staff product knowledge etc

The list is endless but when you put this in the form of a survey in respect of a hotel, then quite a different picture can be formed.

	Attribute	How important is this to you?	How do you rate our business?	Value differential
1	Room size	10	6	-4
2	Bed quality	7	8	+1
3	Furniture and room amenities	5	5	0
4	Friendliness	9	10	+1
5	Hygiene	10	5	-5
6	Meeting area	3	8	+5
7	Architectural aesthetics	7	2	-5
8	Late opening for food and bar	8	8	0
9	Room service	10	10	0
10	Breakfast quality	6	0	-6
11	Free internet	10	10	0
12	Child friendly	0	0	0
13	Pet friendly	0	0	0
14	Early check in	10	10	0
15	Free parking	10	8	-2
16	Automatic check out	5	7	+2
17	Coffee maker in room	5	10	+5
18	Price	5	0	-5
19	Microwave in room	0	5	+5
20	Gift shop	0	0	0
	Total	**120**	**112**	**-8**
	Average	**6**	**5.6**	**-0.4**

This is a form which is completed by a business customer in a hotel in a city centre.

You can deduce from this form the lack of requirement of facilities for children and pets. (An unfortunate link!)

It doesn't matter, and the customers don't care, because it was not important to them. The mark was 0 and the differential was zero.

The third column is not to be exposed to the client. This is for the business itself to calculate. It is this differential which is valuable to evaluate.

From this particular survey it can be seen that the customers do want:

- good room sizes,
- hygiene,
- room service,
- free internet,
- early check in
- and free parking.

These are all marked as '10's in the column, identifying them as being important.

Three are met through room service, free internet and early check in. From this it can be deduced that the room size and hygiene need reviewed. This is a very useful way of concentrating your efforts on what the customer needs.

You are, by default, directing your efforts and those of the team on areas that the customer feels are important and need attention.

You are also gathering data on areas that customers do not feel are important and of course you may be over-excelling in those functions. This is noteworthy in itself. In this example it is the provision of a coffee maker and microwave in the room. These are not considered necessary but marked such that the differential was a 5, along with the meeting room as it is obviously these facilities which are not required.

These are all useful tools for the entrepreneur to understand how they should be directing their team. The entrepreneur will hope that the team can run with the ideas themselves. The entrepreneur will tire of continually thinking up ideas and being a business driver.

Imparting the legendary service concept throughout the organisation is a key to success. This will differentiate the organisation form others in their own marketplace and often it is the little touches that matter. Not necessarily delivering goods on time is as important as backing that service up with after sales care and attention, dealing with faults or breakdowns

Matching and aligning this level of service to the entrepreneur's own standards will create an ordinary organisation in to a great one and also kill at source any frustration festering within the entrepreneur.

It is, be default, making the entire team entrepreneurial, themselves.

5.4 New products and services

The entrepreneur looking in their business (from the outside) will probably never be satisfied with the offering on the table for customers.

The products and services may seem over time to be outdated and tired. The entrepreneur will want to:

- enhance them,

- change them,

- develop them and

- create new offerings.

This is entirely understandable as the entrepreneur will not want to sit still or just be a 'one-trick pony'. This is noticeable, particularly, in terms of product offering.

£££ OUR SURVEY ASKED...

Do you have a niche service or product and if so how important is it to keep to it?

72% answered yes, with a mark of 8.83 in respect of importance to keep to it

However, necessary it is to offer new products or services the entrepreneur must be restrained from investing and researching these to their own end, which could damage the current business by overinvestment or use of vital resources, particularly cash and management time.

£££ OUR SURVEY ASKED...

Have you or do you try other services or products and if so, how important is it for them to succeed?

59% answered yes, with a mark of 6.47 of importance to succeed

Businesses have failed many times because the entrepreneur or business owner has megalomaniacal tendencies. This is a character disorder explained by delusional fantasies of power, relevance or omnipotence. The entrepreneur can be delusional and possess these characteristics, particularly if they have had a track record of success and cannot comprehend, believe nor accept failure. Failure is personal.

However it is bound to happen. The trick or skill for the successful entrepreneur is to know when to stop investing, spending time or chasing the elusive pot of imaginary gold.

It can be very sad and disheartening to see a business try to innovate or re-engineer itself while spending resources which should go on other necessary expenditure or projects. This will inevitably end in disaster.

It is not the entrepreneur who believes in what they hear and what they should develop and that they are indestructible. It is the market determines that fact and that fact alone.

Each new product or service should be tested in terms of the market, its date for delivery and also the likely cost to take it to market. All of these should be understood at the outset and evaluated. The finance to enact this should or could be raised separately or ring-fenced such that the development costs do not impact on the general or sustainable business.

This is a plan followed by successful entrepreneurs who wish to develop, and perhaps develop to the extent that they know that the development may be somewhat fatuous or at a level which does not really enhance the organisation. But if the new development or product is successful it may change the dynamics of the business itself.

The corollary to this is that business **must not stand still**. In the early part of the 21st century any business which stands still is effectively going backwards. The services and products may stay the same in essence but it is the way they are communicated to the customers which may not remain the same.

The impact of technology, the internet and the world of communications means it is essential to adapt to such new technology in order to move forward. To purchase goods from a supermarket only to be told the next day of the latest special offer on your mobile, tablet etc, is digital marketing and customer loyalty in the extreme. Today, however, that and other forms of communication direct to the customer's mobile will evolve and suddenly will become the norm, not the exception.

Therefore it is essential to develop new products and new services.

The entrepreneur has to carry this out but cannot do it wantonly as described above. The method has to be measured and considered in a calm and definitive way.

The board and the non-executive chairperson, as above, need to be able to set out the needs and business requirements to empower a member of the team to research the new offering.

Research and development is essential, it enables the business to establish what it should not invest in and the entrepreneur must realise this and carry the board or the other way around.

Businesses should know their market or niche and become known for operating within that market. To diversify from that may, in the short term be as disastrous a move as with wanton development and unplanned or unbudgeted expenditure. Below is how companies should position themselves:

Low / modest price, with total market focus	Other differentiation, with total market focus
Low / modest price, with niche market focus	Other differentiation, with niche market focus

Does the new product or service fit into the box that best describes the current organisation? If no suitable box can be found, then the activity is outside of the norm and the market perception of the current business.

Understanding the market perception of all of your products, services and offerings is important. It may be that not all of those for your organisation fit in to one box. If not, then closely align the new product to one of yours and see if it matches the box.

Make a list of the products on offer:

Ease of selling product Low demand	Ease of selling product High demand
Difficulty in selling product Low demand	Difficulty in selling product High demand

If the product is easy to sell and there is high demand, then 'go for it' but if it is difficult to sell with low demand, it almost certainly to be a route to disaster.

Throughout this process the entrepreneur must be mindful of the unique selling proposition or known as the 'differential'.

What actually makes his products or services, which may be very common, so special that make customers' buy and buy more and then buy even more. They may buy and buy in quantity and also buy at a price which is considered over and above the market price. Willing buyer, willing seller is mentioned below in the section on 'trade in'; but cannot be better expressed than 'why buy a cup of coffee at one shop compared to another?'. The quality of coffee and the ambience can dictate the price. It may be cool or fashionable to be seen there, and that alone may make the customer feel good. How many now offer loyalty points to obtain your repeat business? What else is on offer in the shop, examples such as newspapers, magazines or wi-fi will surely attract custom for coffee.

Pricing is a sensitive area and adjusting prices or taking market surveys is an extremely good way to test the water. Continually increasing or nudging up prices means there does not have to be a hike, which would jolt the customer into looking around or carrying out their own survey to establish value for money.

The entrepreneur will, from time to time, wish to change pricing structures or even break a promise and compromise the organisation. This may be purely because they need comfort that they are not in a risk business and that the customer is satisfied. The entrepreneur may wake up at night having dreamt that all their customers have left and that their products and services are not required. In that event the board must let the entrepreneur know that the order book and new customers coming in are evidence of a thriving business. The entrepreneur can have doubts.

The entrepreneur is human and will need reassurance.

Selling cheap creates a market but not necessarily a profit and a sustainable business. The right price must be achieved. It is easy to get cold feet but comfort must be taken from the fact that the customer will only be paying the same 'down the road', or if not, a little more but for a lot less service.

The team and the legendary service can overcome pricing differentials.

The need to deliver more products and services is a sound one and spreads the risk. The development must be mindful of the current position of the business, affordable and in line with the overall strategy.

The entrepreneur has to venture to gain.

5.5 Overall strategy

So the entrepreneur has a successful business. They have engaged a board of directors willing to help them. They have products and services and are always looking for new and exciting ways of enhancing the range and offering. The service levels and customer loyalty are second to none.

The business is moving forward with sales increasing, territories and geographical coverage improving with brand awareness.

Financially the results are getting better and better. The profits are increasing and the entrepreneur is faced with the resulting tax bills and perhaps a few people at his door marketing tax strategies to put in place to shelve this tax charge. They can also take out or draw more from the business.

They have choices and a strategy to create and follow.

The strategy must:

- Fulfil the 'want' of the entrepreneur
- Understand where the business needs to be in time periods or 3, 7 or 10 years from now
- Understand the marketplace in which it does and will operate
- Realise that key products will work and some will not
- Create and enhance customer loyalty
- Realise the team required to take it forward

- Establish the capital and funding needed medium term

- Ensure that everyone is understanding what makes the business drive forward

- Put in place a form of reporting and measurement so that the map ahead is clear.

All of these items in the strategy have a future focus.

This is commonly known as a business plan. The creation of a business plan may seem outdated and time consuming but it is not necessarily the exercise itself and the need to demonstrate it that it is important, but the exercise of thinking through what constituent parts and needs are required to fulfil the plan and strategy. It codifies the entrepreneur's thoughts.

It shows the constraints within and on the business, it shows where the team or products need enhancing. Financially it shows where profits are made or not and so on.

The weaknesses of the business will be demonstrated.

These may be:

- Lack of capital

- Lack of credit from suppliers

- Too many customers owing money

- Underperforming owners

- Underperforming staff

- Internal conflicts or poor processes

- Lack of direction and strategy

- Outdated technology

- Lack of marketing

- Poor service

- Missing skills

- No adequate management information

- Retirement and succession issues

- Undesirable customers

- Excessive payroll costs

- High occupancy costs

- Loss-making branches or products

Outside of the business these may be:

- The economy

- Regulatory framework

- Competition

- Demographics

- Energy prices

- Delivery costs

- Pricing war

- New or faster ways of getting to market or production

- Changing market place

- Internet, technology, communications

All of these issues need to be addressed by the entrepreneur and the more the team working with them can understand, recognise and address them and make the entrepreneur aware of them, the better the organisation will be.

The team needs to empathise with business needs and as a result the needs of the entrepreneur themselves. It is not only the entrepreneur who needs to see these and address them, it is the entire team.

The strategy may seem 'all encompassing' but it can only go so far. There are many ordinary businesses in existence providing a good service. They have a strategy of keeping the customer happy, they are not necessarily looking to vastly improve or grow. There is nothing inherently wrong in that.

To have a clear strategy is good. To have a plan and a map of the way ahead is excellent. You do not start a journey to an unknown destination without getting the map out or putting the co-ordinates or postcode into your satellite navigation system.

The plan or strategy, even if well-defined, may change. It may be quicker to go on the A road rather than the motorway, or the toll on the motorway may be preclusive. To hire or rent a new piece of equipment may seem expensive and the improvement in production not that pronounced. It may seem prudent to wait and see.

This is all in the plan or strategy. It is worth reminding ourselves that in our survey 84% of our entrepreneurs had a clear strategy with a mark of importance of 8.1.

A plan or strategy is critical. The entrepreneur will know where they are in terms of the resource required and time through that plan. They will be able to communicate to their staff, the financiers or others where the business is and is likely to be.

They will be more relaxed about their progress and it will be measureable against their own internal wants and needs. This will enable them to empathise with others and the whole process or progress will not only be about them. The progress will be more about the business.

The concept of having a strategy is similar to life. There are certain ages when certain events occur. Such as:

- 0-20, education

- 20-30, live life and look to settle down

- 30-40, settle down, marry have children, develop career

- 40-50, age of expense, career pressures

- 50 on, look to capitalise on all the hard work

- 60 on, retire and rest

- 70 on, remain in good health

- 80 onwards, if you're lucky! 96% of our entrepreneurs were lucky!

This can be similar to the development of a business, which would differ by the speed of the development of a product, market or technology, or simply by taking away constraints such as the requirement of capital.

The life cycle of a business may be to:

1. gain a foothold and establish a presence, to make profits

2. understand the likelihood for progress

3. create a team, new products, new brands, new distribution channels

4. streamline processes and delivery

5. disengage with founding entrepreneur

If the founding entrepreneur cannot do number 5) they will remain stuck within the organisation. The business ages and matures as any person does.

If they cannot do 5) then the entrepreneur is not the entrepreneur they think they are and should retitle themself. They are a general businessperson. This is not a derogatory name - it merely describes the role they play better. The entrepreneur must be willing to change and enable the business to undergo metamorphosis, even if this is without them.

New energy is required to succeed the founding entrepreneur.

A balanced and justifiable, well-developed strategy is critical to success.

> "Boy, did Theo have problems with the car that he bought at Jack's!
> It started off with little things going wrong, for example, a door lock
> needed replacing, some silly bits in the front suspension fell off, you

know the usual sorts of things. Then bigger and more expensive items started going wrong and falling off! First the clutch, then the gearbox, finally the whole transmission. All the while there were plenty of knocks along the way so the car was rarely out of the body shop. So it went on, almost unbelievable. However Theo thought, 'this is not as unbelievable as the fact that the car is just two years old and every SINGLE bit has now been replaced. Hey, look on the bright side – maybe I've got a new car!'"

Is Theo right or is this still the same car. This tale is more often told as the tale of the ship Theseus. This tests our intuition or more importantly of the identity of things or persons over time. Not only is the business changing and developing all the while, but so is the entrepreneur.

If they are not changing and developing and gradually learning throughout the process then again, they fail themselves and the organisation.

The four phases of owning an elephant are a compelling analogy to be quoted at this instance:

Phase 1

You buy a baby elephant. You are bigger than it is, can see a great future with it and foresee no problems. The only concern is that you don't have any skills in managing elephants – but you think that this won't matter and off you go.

Phase 2

The elephant soon grows much bigger than you. You are no longer strong enough to control it and it takes over your whole life. It pulls you along, wreaking destruction in its wake. Standing behind it, it blocks your whole vision and you can neither see or know where you are going. You are so preoccupied by being dragged along by it that you think there is no way to ever bring it under control. It is ruining you and your quality of life. Does this sound familiar?

Phase 3

You are one of the rare people who decides to take advice on how to become a pukka elephant handler. You realise that in order to control your elephant it is no use walking behind it ineffectually holding onto the reins as it pulls you along. You accept that you have to take a wholly different approach and that you have to learn how to manage your elephant to get the most out of it. To do this, you have to know how to sit on top of your elephant, where you can not only see where you are going, but also, with just a gentle touch with your feet on its ears, steer the elephant in the direction you want it to go.

In a short time you are now running the elephant instead of it running you. As a result of accepting that you needed help, and as a result of taking professional advice, it is soon fulfilling your dreams.

Phase 4

Once you have learned how to control your elephant, and it will not take long, you can hire and train your own handler to manage the elephant for you, while you ride in the canopied 'howdah' behind, sitting back and enjoying the view.

How many entrepreneurs get to that position?

To fulfil your dreams you need a strategy and the ability to become a different entrepreneur. Give up the reins and sell.

The entrepreneur has now built a great business from their initial conception and venture. They have enjoyed the journey and they now wish to take some time before selling.

However before that there should be this well-earned time to enjoy the trappings of success along the way. How does the entrepreneur, all consumed by the work required to fulfil his dream, do just that?

CHAPTER SIX

THE SUNDAY DRIVE

6.1 Introduction

The entrepreneur does not spend all of their time working, or trying to make money. They will often enjoy themselves by spending their earnings. They also have to have a social life: to spend time with family, their nearest and dearest, as well as take holidays, time off at Christmas and, from time to time, entertain clients.

To this end the social scene of the entrepreneur, aptly described as the 'Sunday Drive' is interesting to analyse alongside the make-up and character of our subject who we ordinarily meet in the office environment.

This section covers the entrepreneur's spending habits, activities and hobbies, personal life and attitude to health. As mentioned briefly before, sport is an activity which many participate and entrepreneurs are no different. Their interest in sport, probably passively in later life, still continues and any activity is a bonus. Watching and supporting is an excellent second.

The entrepreneur may go in to politics or public life and of course maybe the subject of press and media coverage, as well.

6.2 The social scene

It seemed that the design of Bowater House in Knightsbridge, London, was flawed and detested by many, however it did have a view of Hyde Park. The demolition of this late 1950s building in 2006 was greeted with relief and affluent buyers quickly bought apartments in its replacement building in this upmarket area of West London. It is known as One Hyde Park.

One Hyde Park was developed by the Candy brothers and Qataris and designed by Rogers Stirk Harbour and Partners, the current incarnation of the once-idealistic Richard Rogers practice. The 86 flats, started at £20m with the penthouse selling for £140m in 2010. The building is considered by many as a social catastrophe and a menace towering over Knightsbridge. It symbolises the dark wealth of the elite who claim this area, and the adjoining boroughs, as their own. London is made up of many villages and this is one such audacious tower in a capricious hamlet.

Is any penthouse, in any area, worth that amount of money. It is pleasant to live in central London within easy access of so many facilities but........

To support the price placed on the property the shops in this triangle and maze are all flagship stores, but as you would expect the mark-up in prices abounds without limits. As Alan Whicker once remarked, 'if you ask how much it is, you cannot afford it'. In this environment a pair of ordinary shoes, normally priced at £300, are marked at say £750, a price that bears no relation to their quality, their design or the value of the need to buy the necessity, being a pair of shoes to wear.

They just happen to be in a shop in the right part of town with the right people walking past who do not care about the price. The buyers care about the fact that the luxury goods are an international 'language'. The price does not represent the values mentioned above, the budget of the sensible middle class person, nor a one-off purchase by the well-off aspirational class, but the amount paid by the super-rich who actually do not care about the price. They care about being seen with fashionable apparel and the trappings that one would expect.

That is not the world of the entrepreneur.

The entrepreneur knows what it is like to strive and earn money that so easily can be wasted. It takes one year or more to earn the money and then one split second to spend it on the credit card.

£££ OUR SURVEY ASKED...
Have you ever felt self-indulgent?
36% answered yes

The shop-keepers in Knightsbridge know how to flatter the 'bonus boys and their wives'. The apparel in the shops mentioned above are seen as badges of honour, just as the term 'casino-banking' is seen as a flattering term rather than the insult intended.

The super-rich have no allegiance or connection with wider society. They live in a bubble and, apart from another crash, see nothing that bothers them. They consider their strangely coloured cars, their gated communities and their champagne parties as being all part of the society they have joined. They forget the trials and tribulations life can throw at them. They mix with sports stars and 'a'-listers and are generally the same age. They conveniently forget the future and the long journey that life can be.

It is scary to think that many have such lavish lifestyles but it is a certainty that, at such a rate of spending, they will face financial issues as soon as the income dries up, as their spending will not. Surely difficulties are around the corner.

That is their problem and the issue becomes one whereby lavish spending alienates the ordinary. The normal person cannot comprehend spending on that scale. The spending sprees feed jealousy, distrust, wariness and suspicion, such that the entrepreneur trying to make good can be tainted with the same watchfulness.

The sense of entitlement is beyond quantification. The bonus culture and bankers could not understand why anyone might be mad at them for having:

- nearly destroyed the world economy,

- taken home £30 billion a year of bonuses,

- getting bailed out to the tune of another trillion dollars

- and then lobbied for no regulation afterwards.

It seems that to be allowed to participate in the new society you have to agree to pay over the odds. There seems no alternative. It is this general deterioration in trust that has caused the wider moral belief that to make money is greedy. The fact that, as said earlier, the entrepreneur takes risks to get to that position is clearly forgotten, as the public perception that the bonus culture has overtaken the entrepreneur who may be flush with cash and able to enjoy themselves with a few luxuries.

With failed trades and bad decisions the 'bonus boys and their wives' only risk their reputation and their day job, not necessarily putting in jeopardy the livelihoods of others who work for them or their suppliers dependent on their business.

Unfortunately the excessive or compulsive spender seeks the thrill of not only being able to make the purchase but also to experience that moment in time when they are the 'master' in the situation and the salesperson or the provider of the service is the 'servant'. Much of early drama was founded on the master and servant relationship. Comedy is certainly built upon that relationship.

It is worthwhile pointing out that real business people or entrepreneurs are as angry as ordinary folk (their employees) with the banking crises. It has only made the lending culture on which good business principles are founded yet more difficult to arrange, organise and put in place to employ 'ordinary' folk and use 'ordinary' suppliers, to enable the 'ordinary' economy to turn.

The attitude by the general population to companies and industries, in general, has changed. Telephone companies, energy suppliers, retailers and bankers are all treated with a grim, resigned reflection.

The job of a company employee and particularly the director is still to obey the law, make profits for reinvestment, reward its shareholders and keep abreast of progress. So the sensible entrepreneur, having made their money, spends it wisely and discretely.

£££ OUR SURVEY ASKED...
Do you feel that others are clearly jealous of you?
59% answered yes

If yes, do you feel that they understand the cost to you of being an entrepreneur?
Only 20% of the 59% answered yes

The entrepreneur is surely allowed a comfortable, sensible motor vehicle or two. No-one, other than Buster Keaton, has ever driven two cars at once. Top of the range cars are built with luxurious accessories and there is no reason why a successful businessperson should not enjoy that aspect for their own benefit, or other suitable trappings.

Second holiday homes are also trappings of the wealthy. They can obviously be extremely sensible investments and provide a form of rest and relaxation for the entrepreneur and their family. With modern technology, keeping in touch with the business while away is extremely easy.

The entrepreneur will and should spend. No-one is there to stop them apart from their own conscience, responsibility and overall their integrity.

£££ OUR SURVEY ASKED…

You have decided that there is ample spare cash in the business to draw for yourself. Your passion is sailing. You have always yearned for a particular boat. Do you?

	% answers
Buy that boat or small yacht?	28%
Buy an investment property with a better than expected return?	28%
Give bonuses to key staff?	20%
Keep the money in the bank?	12%
Put the same amount in to a pension fund?	8%
Fund a friend's 'start up business with the appropriate tax relief?'	4%

These are not the statistics of big spenders.

These are the statistics of careful and responsible people who like a little self-indulgence from time to time.

Private jets, yachts, boats and faster cars are trappings of the 'a'-listers more than the entrepreneur but are subtle and less overt than jewellery, clothes and items of personal wear when they are brandished.

Any livestock, one is particularly thinking of race horses, are an expensive luxury. It may be the entrepreneur's hobby but the issue here is that the horse eats and needs to be cared for. Veterinary bills are normally higher than anticipated and are generally unexpected. Horse racing is full of the great and the good. The Lords and the Ladies are supplemented by those addicted to gambling.

Any such hobby or pastime is very relaxing and an interest for the entrepreneur as well as a focal point and place to meet and entertain, but when carried over to be an obsessive, expensive and time consuming occupation it can only become a drain.

Individuals are able to spend their money as they see fit. Entrepreneurs do so too.

It is not only how the entrepreneur spends their time or money but also the approach of the entrepreneur as they do so, which shows them in their 'true light' and whether they respect where they currently are or have come from.

Of course, the entrepreneur has to relate to the golf club secretary, the golf professional, the tennis coach or the organiser of the polo match and even the hotelier and air stewardess.

The rude or the ignorant will try to impose their wealth on those serving them. The master and servant comedy routine continues. The sensible respectful user of these facilities looks after the secretary and the secretariat, the locker man, the bar manager. They know that by issuing respect that good service, and yet better service, will follow. Manners and politeness differentiates the users of these services.

If anyone has stayed in top hotels, or flown first class then it is those extra special trappings and level of comfort which make the pleasure a real noteworthy experience. Even if it is unaffordable today, it is worth saving for a lifetime to experience the thrill of being able to use a private box, or go to an event as a celebrity or first class passenger. Do not deny yourself, but equally take it as it is meant to be, an event. Not necessarily the norm.

As discussed below there are certain addictions in life. Spending and compulsive spending to create a certain image fall within those addictions. It can easily be overlooked that someone with that type of lavish lifestyle may not be able to afford it and may be doing so on borrowed (or stolen) funds.

A final point to make on expenditure and entitlement, which many feel that the bonus culture enables is a lack of respect for outcome. Creating an addiction to computers and their high-speed financial models, mechanistic trading models and bad mathematics, takes away the human aspect from simple transactions.

Entrepreneurs probably think that derivative trading should be illegal and hedge funds banished. What is wrong with buying and selling such items? Money in this former viewpoint is the measure of all things.

Money as Bob Dylan wisely observed doesn't talk, it swears. Do hedge funds and derivatives swear?

The worship of cash now pervades a culture of its own. Go to richkidsofinstagram.tumblr.com, a website of images of young people swigging from magnums of champagne and posing next to private jets. The tagline is 'they have more money than you and this is what they do.' Pleasant approach, isn't it?

Notwithstanding the above, every entrepreneur has the right to spend their money, gainfully earned, on items they want. There is nothing illegal in owning a sports car, nor feeding racehorses. There is something morally wrong in spending money that is not made from profits but loans or investment into the business that is not yours, stopping the business in its tracks. There is also something illegal in spending money that should be taxed. Until a variety of tax efficient schemes are thrown out by the authorities the bonuses earned in that culture is certainly taxed money.

The entrepreneur needs to be able to enjoy an appropriate lifestyle and it is those words that must ring through.

Unfortunately the entrepreneur can be similarly 'tagged'.

Philanthropy is not far away, either.

£££ OUR SURVEY ASKED...

Having drawn the amount out you require and fulfilled your family's dreams and wishes, you develop a philanthropic and social consequence, and wish to give money to charity, what percentage of the excess cash do you give?

	% given
None	24%
Under 10%	56%
Under 50%	13%
Under 75%	7%

The industry serving and surrounding high spenders is an interesting one in itself.

The provision of private jets for hire, boxes at prestigious race meetings and Formula 1 seating arrangements can only be the dreams of the masses. They market these events as such wonderful dreams. You are particularly important if you are sitting on the finish line of the Monaco Grand Prix, or rather wealthy if you are sitting on the finish line of any Grand Prix and extremely important and very wealthy sitting around the green of the 18th hole of a Ryder Cup, for example.

Even the special treats have differential ranks between them. There will always be someone better off than you, don't join the ladder.

As long as the business can afford the dividends or bonuses paid to its star performer or owner, and as long as the correct tax is levied and paid, what is wrong with this type of expenditure? Actually nothing is wrong with it, it just flies in the face of those who cannot afford such luxuries. Remember Owen and his team of workers in the 'Ragged Trousered Philanthropists'.

Being a member of a prestigious sports club, enjoying a nice holiday to celebrate a special event, living in a nice area, are exactly how the proceeds of hard work should be spent.

Affluence and a moderate display of affluence is a perfectly suitable aspiration.

Any entrepreneur should aspire to obtain their chosen luxury. It is obsession, jealousy and indulgence which damages your health.

6.3 Personal life

The entrepreneur will have forsaken many hours of precious time dealing with the development of their business.

This will have undoubtedly meant taking time away from home, travelling, long hours at work and perhaps from time-to-time a few occasions a week meeting and greeting, dining and wining with customers, suppliers, and personalities within the relevant industry and professional advisors. The entrepreneur is networking around the business to the greater good of the business and those within it.

The evenings and possibly weekends spent and the trips away take their toll.

£££ OUR SURVEY ASKED...
Do you feel pleased that you spend so much time on the business?
52% answered yes

This question was designed to get a lower % answer. That is a high percentage to feel 'pleased'.

Family life is not the same. The entrepreneur will not be seeing their children quite as much, not available for every birthday party nor parents' evening and at times it may become a stressful existence as the wife, or husband, needs to understand that the trappings of wealth and/or a better future are not gained easily.

Equally the entrepreneur must recognise that the support from their spouse will 'make' them. They should ensure they are as available as they can be and not fritter their time away with unwanted and unnecessary jamborees. This (along with the hunger developed from trading with borrowed funds) should be a brake on their activities. Golf on a Sunday with chums is good relaxation. A beer with mates on a Friday is good relaxation. However, regular and late, evenings with the wrong friends are a waste of time. They do need to relax but need to understand the most effective ways of so doing.

£££ OUR SURVEY ASKED...
Do you feel guilty that you are away from your family?
32% answered yes

This question was designed to get a higher % answer.

Many the time that through stressful periods the executive spends time away from the family. More than one executive would say that that is the cause of the breakdown of their marriage and the same would say that they should have worked harder on exactly that issue to save their marriage. However, the saving of the marriage can only be carried out by the two within the marriage, it is a team event.

£££ OUR SURVEY ASKED...
Have you been divorced?
32% answered yes

£££ OUR SURVEY ASKED...
If so, do you feel the business was a major contributory factor?
50% of the 32% above answered yes

It is hardly ever a clever move to get divorced, because generally it adds a further dimension to the already stressful existence of the entrepreneur. Divorce happens and the statistics prove it is more prevalent since the late 1960s when there were about 40,000 to 50,000 divorces a year to the 1990s only 30 years on touching 150,000 per year, a threefold increase.

The entrepreneur may find comfort and gratification outside of their marriage. The thrill of being with a new sexual partner is something everyone can experience, not just the entrepreneur. But, when the entrepreneur is engaged in such a time-consuming effort as building a business and worrying about detail or the bigger picture of winning a large new contract then comfort provided by another sexual partner is not only gratifying but potentially an easy option to working at the fundamentals of a relationship.

A full-blown affair consumes time and demands attention as much as the business and the marriage. Why engage in that activity?

This type of transaction could be considered convenient. The use of a casual sexual partner may mean simple gratification. The only outstanding issue is the conscience of the entrepreneur. Under a Christian marriage, the entrepreneur has agreed to love and obey.

This last section may come as a bit of a surprise to those involved in secure loving and monogamous marriages, but the fact is that most in western cities and major towns have strip clubs, lap dancing clubs and where you can find them — brothels. Certain areas in cities are well-known and famous for the provision and selling of sex. It can become an addiction. The entrepreneur may find themselves with the money, the time, the time away from their family and above all an intrigue. It is available.

Let's do some maths; estimates say that there are 300 lap dancing clubs in the UK (not strip clubs nor brothels), with say 30 girls per establishment, resulting in 9,000 lap dancers earning an average of £250 per shift. So, say they work for 40 weeks and they appear four shifts in a week. Then the amount paid to the women, excluding drinks and extras, is worth a staggering £360 million. This proves there are customers for this market.

Contrary to this, the family life of the entrepreneur is very important to the entrepreneur.

This is a comfort area for them, a different view and level from the stresses and strains of everyday life in the office. One in which they can temporarily forget the stresses of the week just gone or the days ahead. They certainly understands their partner's tolerance of the:

- long hours they puts in

- need to be away on occasions

- change of plans at short notice

- occasions they come home stressed on matters the partner has not been involved and yet they may talk at length over dinner unburdening their soul.

Accompanying this, the entrepreneur must respect and trust their partner and also receive this trust and respect in return.

£££ OUR SURVEY ASKED...
Do you take more than 20 days off a year as holiday?
72% answered yes

This statistic alone demonstrates a family person and one respectful of their family's wishes and the ability to move away from the heavy demands of the business and to concentrate on their nearest and dearest.

The mutual respect from the spouse is one of the most important aspects of the entrepreneur's ability to gain inner strength. It is that understanding of the stresses and strains and respect which is probably one of the most important functions of the partner.

It goes without saying that the entrepreneur does not wish to fail, or face bankruptcy and yet events may take that turn. Strangely and perversely, the partner who is so willing to take the upside must accept, alongside the entrepreneur, the downside.

One of the key factors in any entrepreneur's life is whether they have children. If so, their drive will be to enable their children to have a 'better' life than theirs. This is a subjective comment because wealth and money does not always provide a better future and in fact used unwisely it can offer a much worse life.

Money does enable choices to be had.

It is often said that families go 'from rags to riches to rags' in three generations. Some people do not know the true meaning of money. To provide for your children is a very admirable and justifiable cause. The best proof of this is to give them a good education and to provide them with a safe and comfortable environment.

This is not borne out by giving many presents, over indulging at Christmas and birthdays, but to be supportive, to provide and to enable them to have good, sound understanding of the rights and wrongs of life. To have a moral compass that shows them what is necessary to respect others. This will enable them, in time, to become good citizens that others enjoy being with.

Long-standing friends are often the best anyone can have. They prove the case.

Trust is built up over time and is a very worthwhile trait that money actually cannot buy. It can be instilled and taught by examples and role models.

The personal life of the entrepreneur is as important an example of the real inner person, as is their business life.

The entrepreneur will face many choices and dilemmas and in their personal life they need as much focus, commitment and drive as they show in their business life.

The entrepreneur needs to make a success of both to be truly fulfilled.

6.4 Fitness

Entrepreneurs must ensure that they always continue to look after themselves. Health must not be taken for granted.

Stress can do strange things to people and those who suffer from stress and do not take their own health seriously will endure other illnesses as a result.

It will not necessarily manifest itself as a heart attack or a form of cancer, it may show itself in a number of forms. It can be any illness and it would almost certainly be stress-related.

The illness may be frequent attacks of migraines or headaches or even not being able to throw off the common cold or influenza. In that respect recourse to the doctor or the pharmaceutical industry is not always the answer, as easy as it is.

It will be more-deep seated than that. Fit in body, then fit in mind.

The World Health Organisation predicts that by 2020 depression will be the second most common cause of disability worldwide.

At least 1 in 6 people in the UK suffers from a mental health problem at some time in their life. This manifests itself in this being accountable for 25% of all visits to the doctor. Keeping physically fit not only gives our bodies a workout but it ensures that our minds are kept in better shape than they may ordinarily be.

When exercise is taken, biochemical effects occur in the body. Endorphins are released and our serotonin levels (linked to sleep and memory) also increase. Physically, blood flow to the brain is increased and muscle tension is reduced. Psycho-socially exercise improves our body image and confidence. This has a knock on effect to a sense of achievement and being in control.

Physical exercise therefore reduces the risk of depression and inactivity can lead to weight gain and resulting illnesses.

£££ OUR SURVEY ASKED...
Do you engage regularly in a pastime outside of work?
68% answered yes

The entrepreneur clearly needs to regularly exercise to fight stress. This can take the form of light but important exercise such as walking the dog, rambling through fields. To progress and to keep fit this can lead to a much more disciplined and organised exercise routine such as running, cycling or a measured, strenuous programme at the local gym, best done under close supervision from a qualified trainer.

£££ OUR SURVEY ASKED...
Do you exercise regularly (being 2 or 3 times)?
64% answered yes

The fit and physically healthy entrepreneur will be able to face the issues in-hand much better. They will be able to take measured decisions and those awkward or unforeseen events will be taken in the time and order they deserve. They will be able to stand back, go for a run or play a game of golf and then to return to the issue with a fresh view and stance.

Most importantly their approach will not be rash. There will be an air of quiet satisfaction to their daily task. They will have an opportunity to demonstrate their interest and be much more able to communicate as a result. Narrowness of personality will not prevail. 'All work and no play, makes Jack a dull boy'.

Therefore the entrepreneur needs the space and time to do this amongst their otherwise busy life. It is also often said that if exercise is not a priority today, it will become its own priority in time.

Within the world of health there are clearly some vices that will strike down some entrepreneurs more than others. The reason that they will afflict this social class more than the rest would be that they have access to funds to be able to afford such habits.

The vices are addictions to:

- Compulsive spending

- Sex

- Drugs

- Gambling

- Alcoholism

- Smoking

- Poor diet

The first two have been covered above but they can be addictions which lead to personal dramas, most importantly the break-up of relationships and bankruptcy. The next four manifest themselves as serious problems which are slower and not so obviously evident at the outset and can be socially acceptable. The last, diet, is as critical and as vital to good health as the others.

Addiction is the continued use of a mood-altering substance. Its use results in adverse dependency and neurological impairment leading to such altering behaviours.

Would anyone in their right mind subject themselves to such dependency? That is probably the heart of the problem – they are not in their right mind. The addiction often fills a need and desire or satisfies a craving or an inquiring mind.

£££ OUR SURVEY ASKED...
Have you ever had an addiction?
29% answered yes

Nearly one third of those surveyed answering yes, proving an obsessive nature to the entrepreneur.

Psychological dependence occurs when the body has to adjust to the substance by incorporating it into its 'normal' functioning. This state creates the tolerance and withdrawal. Tolerance is the process by which the body continually adapts to the substance and requires increasingly larger amounts to achieve the original effect. The creep in the intake and the consumption of larger volumes makes the social consumption an addiction.

Drugs are classified as opioids, cocaine, cannabis and then perhaps less well-known categories are sedatives, amphetamines, inhalants and substance abuse. Often access to these drugs may start out casually, with peer pressure where it is perceived as 'cool' to take these drugs, yet clearly the continued use, the reliance and then the addiction leads to other, much worse, results. Personality disorder soon results. The entrepreneur ceases to be as measured, focussed and rational. They lose their self-control and as a result the business will not be driven forward.

Withdrawal refers to the physical and psychological symptoms caused by reduction and discontinued use of the substance the body has become dependent on. Symptoms such as anxiety, irritability, intense cravings, nausea, hallucination, headaches, cold sweats and tremors are often the result, but not the only outcomes.

£££ OUR SURVEY ASKED...
Have you ever consulted a therapist for anything?
27% answered yes

Socially acceptable vices consist of:

Gambling

This is not a sin and perhaps even, to own a racehorse, greyhound or even a casino is a passion and desire that may fulfil a lifelong ambition. To gamble is fun, however to gamble regularly may be considered foolish. But to gamble on a regular footing and consider that the next bet will produce the winner and repay all of the previous loss-making gambles is delusionary, to say the least.

The entrepreneur may be led into this as they develop their tolerance to risk and goes about their ordinary business. They may be winning sales contracts and orders without even trying and therefore in that same 'delusionary state of mind' think that they cannot lose on the favourite at 2.15pm.

Gambling is not a substance taken into the body, it produces the same thrill as the spender as discussed above. It creates two effects. The first being the 'negative urgency' effect – the propensity to engage in risky behaviour to create internal distress, commonly known as a 'rush'. There is a response by the individual to this negative stimulus leading to addiction.

The outcome is almost immaterial to the moment of the gamble, and watching the gamble unfold. TV adverts, while they have banned smoking campaigns for health reasons, at the time of writing this book can feature gambling, such that a gamble can be placed on almost any event, at any time, anywhere in the world.

A visit to the website oddschecker.com can lead to you placing a bet on almost any sporting event or outcome. It is not just the 2.15pm nor the football result. Bets can be placed on the next scorer and the number of corners within a match, say. This obviously, was the centre of much match-fixing rings founded and sourced in the Far East and producing astonishing wins and pay outs for those lucky few.

The entrepreneur, with a desire for money, risk and easy wins, will see this as fun at the outset.

The second effect is the 'positive urgency'. This trait has been shown to have a predictive relationship with the outcome. The individual concerned knows the outcome and increases their addiction, and sees no problem with it. While the entrepreneur gambles, they think it is affordable and not an issue in respect of their overall income and expenditure budget. The gambler in these conditions does not think that gambling is differential to their and their family's well-being. The financial loss does not feature.

Drinking

The condition, referred to above, of not recognising the differential to their and their family's well-being is often yet more closely associated with drinking. The drinker who consumes excessive amounts of alcohol seems to cope with the after-effects the morning after and the hangover. It is not a quick entry into alcoholism or dependence.

It is socially acceptable to drink and, particularly for men, as they grow up it is seen to be somewhat manly or macho to consume excessive amounts such that in various social occasions the more that is drunk, the more your peers will think it is acceptable and you are fun to invite. Again, it is marked as a badge of honour to see who can drink the most and still stand upright.

Alcoholic drink is consumed at business lunches, meetings and functions. Again, as with social gambling, there is nothing wrong with such an offering. It may not be as much as mentioned above in the social setting but the consumption of an aperitif and wine and a liqueur with a meal is an extremely pleasant experience.

The issue surrounds the habits of the regular drinker. Much has been written about the use of alcohol as it is probably the most socially acceptable form of substance abuse.

There is the social drinker, who can abstain and knows and obeys the laws in respect of drinking and respects non-drinkers.

There is the problem drinker, which is where the entrepreneur could often find themselves. They drink to get drunk, to dull their senses. They are defensive and justify their drinking as having a good time. At this point, the drinker may have black outs but also definitely mood swings. This drinker will possibly become loud, angry and violent and possibly reclusive, remote and withdrawn. These are not good signs for the entrepreneur and those around them. This would mean that decisions being made may not be rational.

If the problem drinker increases their intake, as a result of the positive urgency and the enjoyment felt from the experience, then they will quickly become the alcoholic.

The alcoholic loses control of their drinking and experiences an inability to keep promises to themselves. They cannot limit their intake or other habits. Excess gambling and sex addiction may recur while they are in this state of disrepair.

The alcoholic:

- spends much time thinking about or planning their next drink

- hides their habit

- denies their habit

- needs to drink when facing stressful situations

- transitions between hangovers to more dangerous withdrawal symptoms

- has or causes major problems, with friends, family or the law and in this instance will almost certainly not be holding down a job at all well or with effect.

If the entrepreneur becomes alcoholic, their business will suffer, not immediately but gradually. In fact the business may be successful and the alcoholic entrepreneur may be able to leave it for continuous periods of time.

This time away will not be spent on a beach sipping Malibu but probably in the dens of inequity in a city centre, drinking and engaging in other activities.

Over time the business will not forge forward and ideas once prolific from this highly respected entrepreneur and businessperson will dry up. Tell-tale signs from those around them start to occur. They lose friends and their marriage, their spending becomes irrational and at times excessive.

Those around the entrepreneur must save them from themselves. Shock treatment is possibly the best, 'it's cruel to be kind' and 'tough love' are sayings that come in to play.

Smoking

Smoking is not necessarily anything other than an unnecessary form of expenditure and the cause of serious damage to the entrepreneurs' health over time, so much so that it seems a nonsensical pastime. The statistics on cancer and other smoking-related early deaths are such that they need not be repeated here.

Tobacco was introduced to Europe in 1559 and by the late 17th-century was not only used for smoking but as an insecticide. Nicotine's effects are different by each report and can be both a stimulant and a relaxant. As a stimulant, some users report it creates alertness and reduces the appetite, raising the metabolism and helping with weight loss. The nicotine in the brain releases many chemical messengers at any one time, increasing concentration, memory, alertness and arousal. The addictive nature is completely understandable and perhaps what is sad is it seems the most difficult substance abuse to rid.

Passive smoking has become the subject of law, with smoking banned from licensed and public premises.

But the entrepreneur needs to have some fun and therefore use in moderation is not a negative.

Diet

What is important, though, for the entrepreneur during these busy hours and stressful days is to understand the need for a proper diet. A poor diet will again lead to weight gain, heart disease, high blood pressure, diabetes, constipation, joint pain, short breath and of course, again, low life expectancy.

Eating too much animal fat such as beef, pork and lamb can lead to weight gain. Unsaturated fats can also increase weight gain. The list is endless and receiving expert nutritional advice is money well spent.

Vegetables and fruit are the main source of minerals and vitamins in the human diet.

Manufactured foods often now include chemical, additives and of course the famous 'e-numbers'.

Certain e-numbers in the form of colourings, preserves, emulsifiers and flavourings are banned in many countries. Spending a period eating unprocessed vegetables or fruit is as thrilling as any dependency or addiction outlined above.

The cleaner the diet the detoxification process provides its own stimulant and better feeling and health.

The ability to control diet, and dependency on any substance will improve the entrepreneur's ability to enjoy the simple things in life and function properly at work.

After all, work is the entrepreneur's biggest 'fix' in life. However, with everything in life, a balance is required.

6.5 In public life

A typical newspaper cutting should read:

'The entrepreneur and businessman John Smith returned from a happy two week holiday in Spain on Saturday. His children looked extremely happy and rested after their break and are looking forward to the new school year, despite having exams to sit in a few months. John and his wife were heard to comment how well their holiday had gone. John runs his own business 'New ideas' a digital media business based in Milton Keynes.

The business employs 25 staff and is up-to-date with all necessary payroll, personal and corporate taxes. The accounts, personal tax returns and annual returns are filed well within time. His suppliers are paid after 30 days without fail and he is looking to take on two more staff. As a result of the excellent service that his customers receive they have been able to recommend his services, and the testimonials on the website bear that out, and as a result he is happy to report that the business has grown at an average of 12% for the past three years.

The business experiences little in terms of bad debts. John himself takes modest drawings from the business and while he enjoys driving a luxury car and is a member of a sailing club, he feels this is just and fair reward for the work and efforts he has put in to the business.'

Unfortunately this type of reporting is extremely rare, albeit a very common event in life and a wonderful story to tell.

There are many such couples and many such honest businessmen, trying to simply do well. This reporting, apart from not selling newspapers, is not interesting to readers who want intrigue, odd or weird events, and therefore is not front page news.

What is required for the front page is the latest news or report on the entrepreneur who everyone thought was the model family man and successful businessperson, but who became:

- the bankrupt

- the philanderer

- the murderer or criminal

- the double dealer, claiming for insurance for stolen goods or arson

- the swindler and abuser of their position, such as always promising the delivery of goods and taking money upfront and not delivering those goods

- the abuser of vulnerable people by taking their Christmas savings, for example.

This sort of story sells papers and enables the reader to relate with the tormented victims. The story enables the reader to be filled with disgust and disdain for the tormentor, the abuser and the paper will call them 'the entrepreneur who……'

The public perception of the entrepreneur is made worse by this media coverage.

The media seem to enjoy making an example of this supposed 'abuse of power', 'greed' and the 'master and servant' relationship.

Entrepreneurs will not be seen as the sensible, tax-paying, responsible, mature, compassionate and solid businesspeople good for society, unless the media change their reporting.

No story tells of the honest, hard-working and responsible and passionate entrepreneur who makes their living and lives their life accordingly.

That type of story does not sell magazines or newspapers.

The public persona is very different to the private person.

CHAPTER SEVEN

THE 'TRADE IN'

7.1 Introduction

The success of the business and the ability to 'earn a living' are key primary deliverables for anyone starting a business. However, that milestone is probably passed at an early stage once the turnover and sales of the business are sustainable. As profits are achieved on a regular basis, other objectives appear on the horizon.

The final leg of the journey is the eventual sale of the business by the entrepreneur, thereby relinquishing or releasing their majority interest in its ownership. The financial incentive is very attractive.

Between these points there may have been sales of equity to enable cash to be invested in the business to allow it to grow and develop. However its eventual realisation for the entrepreneur to enjoy the fruits of their labour can be substantial.

As has been written many times: five times a business worth £1 million is easier to achieve than 10 times a business worth £500,000. The more valuable the business then the less pressure on the multiples needed to achieve a certain value. Multiples will be discussed later.

So effectively, strategic inward investments at certain points in the lifetime of the business and at certain multiples allow the entrepreneur to conceptually view the value of their remaining shareholding and therefore, by default, their eventual exit.

These strategic sales also allow the entrepreneur to maximise their value on exit and time the exit to their best advantage, unless other events take over.

The sale of the business does not just happen. A considerable amount of work is required to enable the business to be sold. In fact this may be the most difficult achievement, with the biggest 'stretch'. Often the entrepreneur will be out of their comfort zone and facing this as a 'one-off' event. So much hangs on it.

To trade in the business is a lifetime's achievement wrapped up in one transaction. The 'baby' is being sold, like one's first car, the car you probably learned to drive in – it will be a memorable day. Emotion must not be in the way.

7.2 Grooming for sale

The entrepreneur is feeling very proud of themselves. They have grown their business and operated it for a number of years.

Let us imagine it has sustained at least one recession, undergone the compliance of a few years of external audits and possibly had one or two rounds of investment from outsiders.

The business has clearly stood the test of time.

It is obvious that the business has value, and as far as the entrepreneur is concerned anyone can see that. The problem is that the value attributed to the business by the entrepreneur has a number of emotional factors that others may not see. The entrepreneur will undoubtedly value it higher than the market is willing to pay unless in exceptional circumstances there is a particular angle that the buyer sees.

These circumstances can sway the buyer either way to perhaps increase or even decrease the sales value, but in essence to decrease the value it may be that there exists:

- stable senior management – not likely to conform with the new organisation

- a sales force – duplicated in certain areas

- a customer list with few new accounts

- products which need new designs

- an under-utilised production facility

- systems and processes to be updated

- lack of good financial control

However, while these may seem negatives to any buyer they can themselves make the business attractive to a particular buyer.

The term 'willing seller, willing buyer' is most relevant at this stage. The issue being that everyone will see some beauty in something. It is not all about how it is packaged. It is not all about size and profit.

Loss-making businesses have been sold many times over for large sums of money. For example businesses in old, perhaps, even tired, sectors have value due to 'know- how', customer contacts and databases.

It can be strange what people buy. You only need to walk around car boot fairs, or think of that odd house for sale which was next to the railway line with the motorway roaring past to realise that beauty is not only in the eye of the beholder but that everything has a price, even a business.

Hence the business does not necessarily need to be 'groomed for sale', but to maximise the price and to enable the business to find the right buyer and allow the entrepreneur every chance of success, it does need to be put into a state for sale.

The negatives mentioned above (and others) need to be taken out of the equation. This would ensure the best chance of finding a suitor willing to offer the right price and within the time frame the entrepreneur needs.

This does not mean that all the work is carried out in-house by the current management to enable someone to come along and just pick up the pieces. Careful thought needs to be put into the strategy to enable the business to be sold at its maximum price.

It takes a number of steps and the entrepreneur needs to be alongside all of these steps, understanding why they are making every move and the potential cost.

The steps are:

- Defining a strategy

- Making the entrepreneur dispensable

- Ensuring due diligence is minimal

- Leaving something in the deal

Defining a strategy

A full strategic review and planning process needs to be undertaken. If the entrepreneur does not wish to carry this out, doubt must be placed on how serious they are about actually selling their interest or business.

This should encompass a review of the nuts and bolts of the business, to discover which items in the activity may be attractive to a potential buyer. One of the key areas would be to review the market place and to be able to target potential buyers, other than management.

One of the key processes that can be uncovered during this process may be termed 'equity layers'. In other words, were the entrepreneur to carry on longer, and perhaps with further investment, the business may become more valuable. Time and investment could produce key add-ons or 'equity layers', these may take the form of:

- management

- processes and systems

- intellectual property or development

- better business models or enhanced contributions

- creating a better brand

- enhancing the distribution channels

All of the above would make the business a bigger entity and thereby more valuable.

Is the entrepreneur capable of making this happen?

Within any of these processes it may be that the entrepreneur sees a short-term target to buy before selling. This would involve activity such as identifying a smaller business to buy or a target which may merely have turnover (adding critical mass) and enables the entrepreneur to carry on and not sell in the foreseeable short-term future. This is effectively envisaging a clearer route and a neater or simpler way of exiting in time to come.

Hence, the strategy and process must allow the entrepreneur time to understand exactly what they have for sale and perhaps more importantly how it should be sold.

The example in the preceding paragraph is designed to show that the entire process to prepare for sale may not just involve matters within the current business.

Many businesses take on capital investment without a clear view of where it needs to take them. This strategy review should not allow that to occur.

Financial modelling, with clear financial forecasts that include 'what if' analyses, also allows the entrepreneur to understand a true value the business.

This could be in the form of a pure profit and loss or cash-flow forecasts, relating back to multiples or earn out. The multiple or earn-out is what a prospective purchaser is prepared to pay for the profit stream in their own new organisation.

Therefore, expenditure at this stage on a consultancy project should be won back many times in the future.

The entrepreneur has backed their own confidence in their own ability to date, as we have understood in the previous chapters. This activity therefore has no risk, other than a cost, but is an obvious enhancement to this vitally important and critical project.

Many entrepreneurs do not undertake this process, though. They have an idea of the value of the business but not formally. This process, even though the business may not eventually be sold, can still be considered a valuable exercise. It is looking at the business from the outside in.

The final piece of the strategy would be to identify the potential acquirer. This is not a simple advert in the latest trade magazine to seek such a target.

The buyer will quickly identify themselves through market research or even be on the books of a 'broker', actively seeking acquisitions.

The potential acquirer must have:

- cash available to do the deal

- cash available for the working capital required

- intent and desire to take over

- adequate management

- 'great plans', a subjective comment but worth making

- be a safe pair of hands for the existing customers, suppliers and employees.

The first three set out on this list are critical. The others mentioned on the list, not so important, but valuable for the continuation and especially so if there is deferred consideration.

The responsible entrepreneur should have an 'unwritten' tri-partite agreement between themselves, their customers and their staff.

Making the entrepreneur dispensable

Dealing with the actual transaction is not for this book but the entrepreneur needs to understand that the future is not their problem. This is the start of the mental realisation by the entrepreneur that they need to make themselves dispensable from the business.

The business has to operate without them. The key words in that sentence are 'to operate'.

The entrepreneur may be able to continue as a figurehead or to present their image and presence, perhaps even continue to sell and market the business. This is often quite understandable and common.

The entrepreneur has been linked to the business by an unseen and imaginary umbilical cord for years. This cannot easily be 'cut' overnight. Often it is and there are good reasons for this. It may be that the new organisation knows that the entrepreneur:

- would not fit into the new organisation,

- cannot travel to the new organisation or there is no wish on their part to be part of it,

- has no need for a handover,

- the business is moving on at such a pace the entrepreneur is superfluous to requirements.

All of these actions make the entrepreneur redundant.

The entrepreneur has to realise that his day has been and gone. The sale and their exit does not ordinarily mean that they face retirement as we will see later in this chapter, but that their input into this particular business is no more or vastly reduced.

Part of the skill required by this process will be to ensure that the entrepreneur's management input is reduced. It is highly likely, unless the sale is to a business that wants it to operate as an autonomous subsidiary rather than integrating it in to the new organisation that the entrepreneur will, in fact, no longer be required.

What can the entrepreneur do now, so as mentioned before, the ability for the entrepreneur to promote the business is probably the best short-term route forward. It is suggested that part of the process will be to groom the business but also the entrepreneur into this role. Given that this may be a key element of the sale it is essential for the entrepreneur to understand and be ready for this event and undertake the concept with the importance it deserves.

They cannot nor must not meddle or be involved or criticise the new management's decisions.

Effectively they should 'take the cash and run for the hills'.

This is a harsh statement but meant as such because unless the entrepreneur recognises this is their new role and future function then the handover will not work, for themselves practically nor mentally and for the acquirer practically.

The extraction from the business can be before the sale takes place and this can take the form of:

- not being present at management meetings or some board meetings,

- devolving more responsibility to others,

- allowing future plans to be in the hands of local management,

- not being present nor involved with interviews for future employees.

Clearly this demonstrates that they are not too involved in the future of the business but it also shows that the business can run without them. This will greatly enhance the entrepreneur's reputation with the acquirer as it shows that:

- the business is not centred around the entrepreneur,

- the entrepreneur has allowed others to participate

- and also more importantly that they can walk away at some stage within a pre-agreed timescale.

This allows the entrepreneur time to concentrate on matters in hand such as promoting the business.

The worst case scenario is just walking away, never to be seen again.

Ensuring due diligence is minimal

Obviously when a business is sold, due diligence is an integral part of that process.

The acquiring company has to ensure that what they think they are buying, they are in fact doing so. Also that on acquisition there are no hidden surprises particularly unknown commitments and unforeseen contingencies along the way attaching to the business. This would be the case were the acquirer to buy the shares of the business as that is buying the business in its entirety.

The process of acquiring assets is a lot simpler. The acquirer needs to ascertain that the seller has title and that there are no encumbrances, such as mortgages or debentures to those assets.

The action of acquiring the shares could be considered simpler in as much as the whole package comes along but contingencies, as mentioned above, may include:

- sales contracts with termination clauses for a variety of reasons, one may be the sale of the business

- suppliers anxious to protect their own intellectual property

- leases for equipment and premises

- premises with dilapidation clauses

- employees' rights

- contingencies or letters of intent

- claims experienced under professional indemnity insurance or products liability

- bad debt experience being latent customer dissatisfaction.

The list is not endless but care must be taken by the acquirer to be aware of the possibilities of there being a contingency and if so, that it is within the bounds of normal business, thereby acceptable, and does not preclude the deal to be carried out.

This activity impacts on the 'sensible' entrepreneur, who is a wary seller. The more they can groom the business for sale, not the month, or even the year before sale but as they go along, the easier it will be for them to sell when the occasion arises.

The acquirer may have carried out these duties and activities before and will clearly see that the due diligence process is relatively straightforward as the information required is not only at hand but transparent, such that the acquirer can make informed decisions on what is given and provided to them.

All sales and customer contracts must be prepared and written in the correct legal and up-to-date form. The business and the customer must be correctly protected in most events. Payments must be made by the customer to the selling business under these terms and all issues must be fair and reasonable and dealt with correctly and more importantly in a timely manner.

There must be no onerous conditions within any paperwork that make the deal unlikely to succeed. Management information must be regularly produced, reports on issues and problems must be made in a timely manner to the board. Insurance must be adequate and up to date, and claims reasonable if any.

All of these point to a business with good house-keeping, monitored and controlled in a very professional manner.

There may be events in the past or even recent history that do not demonstrate this. That is fine but it must be apparent that the business, and the entrepreneur took these on board and dealt with them properly.

The input from the entrepreneur is critical at this stage. They have to realise the importance placed by an outside party on this. It is no good at this stage saying 'we have always done it like this'. That is dismissive and likely to scupper any deal at the outset. The legality of any activity, the paperwork and audit flow are essential to the deal progressing.

As mentioned before this 'audit' of the paper trail is a worthwhile exercise even if the business is not sold.

Leaving something in the deal

Any sale has to be to the right buyer. The term 'willing buyer, willing seller' has already been used in this chapter but it is extremely relevant.

When a simple house conveyance is carried out is it normally because the sellers wish to move. They may wish to move to another area because of the employment prospects but generally because the house is too big or too small during the lifetime of the family.

The house changes 'shape' as the family develops. Or rather the family's requirements of the house change as the family grows up. Most couples start with a two- or three-bedroom house or flat and then may move to a bigger four- or five-bedroom house as they wish to start or have a family. At some stage the house and/or garden will become too much as the family grows up and moves on. The house may need improvement, redecoration or an extension. There is much work that can be done to it to improve its value.

So something should and must be left in the deal for the next person.

The acquiring company must see something that they admire.

Alan Shearer was the most successful forward-playing footballer of his generation and a likely target for the big clubs challenging for the league title. The press had him 'nailed on' to be sold by Blackburn Rovers to Manchester United in 1996. Newcastle United stepped in and bought him. This was always considered a backward move for Alan, because Newcastle United may not challenge for honours year in and year out like, say, Manchester United but Alan maintained he had gone home, even to his spiritual home as he was a boyhood fan of Newcastle United.

Many in the game considered that while this broke the bank for Newcastle and the transaction did not seem to progress Alan's career, as it was an unfashionable club, Newcastle United made the move because without him they would have been further behind Manchester United.

The acquisition was as defensive as it was progressive.

Something has to be left in the deal for the next person. It may be a positive issue or it may be stopping a competitor gaining, as demonstrated above. The purpose of every deal may not be clear at the outset.

Much has been written about the financial crisis that hit during 2007/08, culminating with the inquisition into many of the acquisitions by the Royal Bank of Scotland ('RBS') acquiring ABN Amro. The Treasury Select Committee has severely criticised the FSA (now FCA) judging it a 'serious indictment' of the former management of the city regulator. The £49 billion deal is one of the factors that led to the illiquidity of the acquirer RBS that led to its £45 billion bailout by the British taxpayer. Amazing how the figures match.

What happened here? Why did RBS think this was such a good deal, why didn't management within RBS stop it, and why didn't the FSA intervene? These are questions which remain unanswered and are not the subject of this book.

What is the subject of this book is the internal drive of the entrepreneur to carry out this deal – did the entrepreneur or entrepreneurs (the management of the acquiring bank) really believe that there was merit in the deal?

The lack of merit in the deal had such far reaching consequences that it effectively brought a bank down, Many said that it is surprising that the entrepreneur agreeing to the deal had the ability to do such a thing, let alone persuade the management and have it passed by the regulators. Ego?

There is a 452-page report from the enquiry chaired by Lord Turner on the failure of the deal which is said to have lead to RBS's failure. These include:

- significant weaknesses in RBS's capital position, as a result of management decisions and an inadequate global regulatory framework

- over-reliance on risky short-term wholesale funding, which was permitted by an inadequate approach by the regulation of liquidity

- concerns and uncertainties about RBS's underlying asset quality because of the fundamental analysis by the FSA

- substantial losses in credit-trading activities, which eroded market confidence and both the bank and the regulator underestimated how bad the losses were

- the ABN-Amro acquisition took place with 'inadequate due diligence'

- an overall systemic crisis in which banks in worse relative positions were extremely vulnerable to failure. RBS was one such bank.

One might say that people were playing with others' money. The board game 'Monopoly' teaches the theory of not going bankrupt or buying too much property, keeping liquid assets such as cash in case have to pay a fine or accidentally land on the 'go to jail' square and have to pay £50 to get out.

No one has landed on the 'go to jail' square in this example and if they did who would pay for their time before release, the British taxpayer again?

The example shows the need for any acquirer to carry out not only due diligence but also to understand the fundamental reason why the acquisition is being made.

The acquisition cannot simply be termed megalomaniacal behaviour. Megalomania is explained as having a psychopathological disorder characterised by 'delusional fantasies of power', relevance or omnipotence.

What was the benefit in RBS buying ABN Amro? This will probably be a business masters degree examination question in years to come when it is consigned to the textbooks.

The acquirer should look to the deal as adding to their:

- Brands

- Market share

- Geographical area or distribution channels

- Production facilities

- Management structure

- Intellectual property

- Profits

These are obvious reasons but often overlooked.

As with Alan Shearer defensive acquisitions are extremely sensible.

Any entrepreneur acquiring a business because it pampers to their psychopathological needs is doing it for the wrong reasons. It obviously occurs and in the biggest deals will lead to the most calamitous of circumstances.

There has to be something left in the deal for the acquirer – demonstrated and manifestly shown as such. It is then down to the acquirer to maximise that opportunity but it does have an effect on price and the multiples that could be achieved.

7.3 The exit

Having decided to exit, the deal should be easy to execute. Having groomed the business for sale, with all the necessary due diligence, the deal may be easy to do.

Leaving the business may not be so easy or so straightforward as emotions come in to play.

The prerequisite to any deal is the value that can be achieved. That pound sign will obviously attract, and more importantly, focus the mind of the entrepreneur.

The deal may not be the best on the table, nor at the level that the entrepreneur expected. However it may have other attributes in respect of timing or continuity. Businesses survive because of both those aspects, and in the future they may:

- require a new cash injection

- need to be taken to a new level

- require the continuity which suppliers and employees can provide

- require new efficiencies and passion, due to the entrepreneur's own personal circumstances.

The act of selling to management is often seen as negative because the cash is not necessarily readily available and it may take time to receive all of the proceeds. However it may be that more cash is forthcoming or the same amount at least as with any other deal to a third party because of relative uncertainty with new owners and performance clauses within the sale contract.

The new management will undoubtedly work for the benefit for the company once it is under their ownership as their own livelihood is dependent upon it. They are also now developing the firm for their own eventual sale to make a turn on it.

So the exit occurs.

The entrepreneur has to understand that the act of signing the contract and the exchange thereof is their parting 'party piece'. There is little left to do, apart from collect payment, promote the firm or give advice – when asked.

The entrepreneur is selling their 'baby' and allowing it to go out into the wild to fend for itself. The lion cub departs the lair and has to make its own way.

Ordinarily any entrepreneur should not continue with a remaining interest in the business unless it is a minority interest, nor expect much from that interest soon, the business is sold and they have no control. The interest may be realised at a certain date, but why hang on?

It may be that the exiting entrepreneur is leaving it to their business partner, especially if a 50:50 partnership, say, has broken down. The valuations in these circumstances are difficult as one party will value the business higher and want more to go, while the remaining interest will have to earn the pay-out.

In these circumstances 'no-blame divorces' are extremely valuable clauses to include in a shareholders agreement. The no-blame divorce allows one party to offer their shares to the other at a certain value. If the party receiving the offer does not accept then the party making the offer has to accept the price offered. This stops unrealistic and time-wasting conversations, and allows parties to part amicably at the right price.

Shareholder agreements and a mechanism to value shares, at the outset of a business are critical (yet rare) for any business with more than one party involved.

The exit is an emotional time for the entrepreneur. Immediately they have been stopped in their tracks from working.

The worries and stresses and strains of ownership have gone.

Empathy with them is essential, at this time. Respect as they depart is paramount.

7.4 New plans, serial investor?

The entrepreneur has his cash. Hopefully it is cash, not shares in the new company or much in the way of deferred consideration, unless it is bankable it is worthless.

Then the entrepreneur has choices:

- retire and/or stop work,

- follow their dreams and do something completely different,

- look for another opportunity,

- or look to become a serial investor or angel with the knowledge gained,

- look to manage their investments – while tending to the garden.

Retirement is there for the selling entrepreneur of a certain age. To be able to follow the dream such as playing golf or fishing or perhaps doing the things that were always affordable but there was never enough time.

Taking time to travel, write or paint are always suitable substitutes to working. Work is as much occupational therapy as providing a way to sustain oneself.

However, building your own business is not relative to the time and hours at the 'shop', 'mining at the coal face' or 'spent in the office', the seller deserves rest because of a weight of responsibility that cannot be measured and takes its toll is relieved. This refers to the responsibility carried by having to meet the wages' bill, dealing with all the issues with suppliers and customers etc paying government taxes and all the compliance which a business owner today faces. It will only get worse.

The entrepreneur deserves a rest.

The buck has always stopped with them. Any failure is theirs, so success should be too. To go back to those stresses may not be the most sensible route and often the hunger and desire is missing.

The entrepreneur may seek other opportunities. Often the entrepreneur may be proven to be a 'one trick pony', unable to turn their skills to another project. As a result they fail and quickly burn their gains from the first success. It may be that they feel that they still need to prove themselves.

This is tantamount to a form of gambling but the entrepreneur will want to continue, albeit blind to the lack of progress, because they will undoubtedly not give the new project the time or patience they gave the original one. Perhaps they enjoy the master and servant relationship, too much.

The entrepreneur will want to get to the end game quicker.

This is testimony to a psychopathological flaw, in a sense, and totally unnecessary. Yes, they may be successful in a new venture but undoubtedly it will be success through another route. They will not have the 15 years to spend as mentioned at the outset of this book.

The best route would be to invest in one or a number of developing businesses and allow the management in those businesses use their desire, hunger, passion and vision to drive the individual businesses forward, not to get in the way. However, they have to be strong again in as much as any business always devours cash. They must not be seen just to be a funder of last resort. Their capital is seed capital and should be treated as such. Strict adherence to a business plan is critical in this event.

This route as a 'business angel' should be fun.

They can:

- attend board meetings,

- provide advice,

- mentor directors, (the new business may have younger operators)

- deal with and fulfil projects,

- promote or represent the business.

The entrepreneur should keep away from day-to-day management.

The 'business angel' should understand the business in which they invest. On this occasion the 'business angel' should also be able to lose the investment without hurt.

All of this will be good use of the experience and expertise gained from actually doing it the first time around.

If the entrepreneur wants to actually manage their investments by seeing them develop, better or for worse in cash form or as marketable securities, then that too can be of interest and a hobby alongside playing golf, bridge or other restful pastimes.

It is often the subject matter of conversation at golf clubs how 'such and such' a share is doing – boring but true.

The entrepreneur, turned investor, should then recall some quotes and stories from the great French philosopher and writer, Voltaire:

'Each player must accept the cards life deals him. But once they are in hand, he alone must decide how to play the cards in order to win the game.' So if the entrepreneur wins and sells, do not moan, bemoan or regret losing the second time around, there will be other opportunities.

Having won the game, Voltaire allows his hero Candide to settle down on the outskirts of the Muslim city of Constantinople to 'tend his own garden' – in other words to mind his own business. After witnessing some horrifying episodes of religious intolerance and political oppression Candide decides that the best thing to do in the world is to settle down, live peacefully with his neighbours and produce something of value. This is fulfilled with his own garden. To watch it grow and enable him to sustain himself and others with its produce.

Gardens are seasonal and there is always something to do. The entrepreneur will understand that each plant needs the right soil, position, sunlight and feeding to give it every chance of growth. They did that with their own business and capably took it to market.

Gardens produce flowers and fruit annually, the entrepreneur may not be so successful each time.

CHAPTER EIGHT

WHO CAN USE THIS MANUAL?

8.1 Introduction

The purpose of starting up in business is to be successful. Otherwise, as mentioned before, there seems little point. Success is measured first by earning a living and then perhaps by earning super-profits and selling your business, such that you retire with money in the bank.

Money in the bank is a wonderful safety net for financial security in later age.

Therefore who should use this book to educate themselves in the practices of the entrepreneur?

The answer is those who wish to become an entrepreneur and those who deal with entrepreneurs, and most importantly those who back entrepreneurs.

8.2 Becoming an entrepreneur

Wherever you are growing up in the Western world, money is the key to:

- firstly, survival – meeting the weekly food bill
- secondly, luxuries – experiencing a great Christmas or summer holiday and

- thirdly – to take away any worries about the future.

A comfortable lifestyle can be had with the adequate provision of money.

In a third-world country, money is important but not so important as a day-to-day living can be scratched from the land. This is dissimilar to the Western world where a benefits culture has replaced the need to work, if basic essentials for day to day living cannot be earned.

Luxuries are often not available to the ordinary person in the third world. Many have not travelled outside of their native country.

Needs in retirement or ill health are mostly catered for by the family.

So differentiating the western world form those in a third world country the driving force, despite the maturity of the economies is to earn money. Earning a living is almost a pre-requisite to anyone with any form of education. There happens to be a multitude of professions or trades in which to do this.

Luxuries abound and can also be experienced such as a memorable Christmas and/or a summer holiday. They are within most people's grasp if they have work. Simple savings plans can provide for the cost of that luxury over a period of a year.

Saving or catering for the future is more difficult as pension plans have become the subject of much rancour during the past 20 years. Savings and pension companies have not been able to fulfil the forecasts they once set and the provision of commissions and fees running such schemes have brought the annuity income down for the prudent saver.

More reliance is therefore put on the state unless someone in employment is able to inherit, invest wisely and invest in alternative structures such as assets which may produce capital and investment income. These will need to be managed by the investor, which is part of the attraction of the pension company as the worry and decisions are subcontracted but at a cost. Also, unlike pension contributions which attract tax relief, alternative investment needs careful tax planning.

Making these decisions will impact on the lifestyle afforded by the employee. Saving for retirement will become yet more difficult in years to come than it is today. As mentioned in the opening chapter, wage stagnation was mentioned to be a driving force for new entrepreneurs to create businesses and to try to make their fortune. With that concept to the fore another driving force will be to hope that their asset, being their business, will become their pension or at least some funds partly sufficient for retirement

So to become an entrepreneur and to be successful at that, can take all of these three needs away. They are: the need to live, the enjoyment of experiencing luxury and the need to save for old age.

Obviously, as an entrepreneur, earning a day-to-day living is taken as given, luxuries will be affordable and time required to enjoy them may not be so readily available. The successful entrepreneur will use excess earnings or profits to enter into alternative investments, to spend on adequate pension provision and the successful sale of the business will ensure cash assets sufficient not to worry about the future.

Becoming a successful entrepreneur clearly could have tremendous financial benefits. It is not just the status of becoming respected as such a person that has sufficient draw to make the effort worthwhile.

Becoming an entrepreneur can be by default. Entrepreneurs may trip over their idea or product by accident and wonder how to deal with this hidden jewel. Some may not even see it and have to be guided towards the 'mecca' of putting the idea and all it entails in to practice. They are not so lucky. They do not see the opportunity staring at them.

Accordingly we may be writing about celebrities who have earned money from playing sport at the highest level, singing or acting and who then look to invest in business. They may not know much about the target investment yet consider themselves entrepreneurial enough to be able to make that investment.

Without expert knowledge in their field of investment they would surely just be considered 'business angels' rather than entrepreneurs with their own ideas and services.

Some do, but they will be starting with clear, differentiating factors: fame, which can lead to an immediate market share; and perhaps the most difficult resource of all, money. Therefore if they are putting their name to a new but tried-and-tested product such as clothing or fashion, it can be an immediate hit, until their name becomes tired. Fred Perry sportswear was the rage in the 1940's and still is, but obviously other new labels endorsed by sportsman from a more recent period are now in the market.

Without those head-starts the 'ordinary' entrepreneur has to battle to succeed.

To make the 'first million' is considered the hardest and yet possibly for many entrepreneurs the most satisfying. However, the same concepts or analysis are required by the entrepreneur whether it is their 'first', 'second' or 'last million'.

Even the same analysis is required and should be appreciated for any form of investment for their savings.

To become an entrepreneur they need to make the most of their skill set, engage others at the right time and learn new skills. Otherwise they may face failure.

Not every entrepreneur is successful and the downside of committing hard-earned cash or inherited assets to the bank or lender or other financial organisation can mean that failure has a catastrophic effect on the entrepreneur, his livelihood and family.

All could be lost. The entrepreneur operates under such pressure. They deserve the payback but is it really something that the ordinary person, without the necessary skill set should really entertain?

The budding entrepreneur needs to be true to themselves to recognise why they are engaging in such an exercise. It has risks.

The skills referred to above must be evident otherwise the entrepreneur will fail. Perhaps the greatest route to failure is over-reliance on the ego. The ego of the entrepreneur can often over-shadow reasoned argument given by others around them. The entrepreneur may be blinded by the sole reason for their success, or early success and follow a route that can lead to disaster.

The upcoming entrepreneur must understand that there is a lot to be learned. Winning on a management course, or taking a relevant degree is far from the practical steps of handling a real live situation of an unhappy customer or dissatisfied employee.

It is worthwhile for the entrepreneur to cut their teeth on a failure or even be engaged in a similar organisation to see how others do it before they venture out on their own or risk their own money (and house).

This apprenticeship is invaluable.

Why do trades give youngsters apprenticeships? Why were there livery companies applying early trade standards? This was to enable the skill and knowledge to be passed on.

The common view that a business studies course is a suitable substitute to learning about entrepreneurship is unfounded. However, it will give budding entrepreneurs a basic knowledge of certain areas in business they may not already know or possess. It is a good second to real life experiences.

The skills referred to before in the sections on the 'basic model' or 'optional extras' regarding intelligence and personal traits cannot be taught easily.

Effectively, if you wish to become an entrepreneur - it is not that simple.

An entrepreneur does exist within you if you are self-employed. However taking those next steps to engaging employees is a step too far for many. One to five employees can be closely monitored and handled but as soon as there are a number of rungs of command or when the entrepreneur may not know of everything going on in their organisation then they need to develop a whole new vision.

A customer may contact them about an issue which they are unaware of or cannot handle technically. The entrepreneur must be able to listen, understand enough to decide how to deal with it, allow the right person to deal with it, and follow it up until the matter is resolved. The greatest attribute will be that the customer uses the business again.

Reliance on others is a skill in its own. Imposing adequate monitoring procedures is essential.

Trust is the key to the success of the entrepreneur and ensuring those around them are empowered to fulfil their goals within the safety of the entrepreneur's organisation.

To become an entrepreneur needs judgement and vision, not least maturity. This does not preclude the young. The cost can be great to your health and family and you need to give the required time to any venture. Time is the most precious commodity.

Do you have what it takes to become an entrepreneur? The five major characteristics are set out in chapter 9.3.

8.3 Dealing with an entrepreneur

The idea for this book came on a course designed for partners in accounting firms. One of the key questions was succession. The course questioned whether budding senior managers, who were to become the future or next partners and thereby the rainmakers and fee winners, able to 'cut the mustard'. Could they relate to the clients effectively?

At this conference the current managing partners were questioning if the senior managers had enough gravitas, enough experience and enough social graces to convince the client entrepreneur or business owner that they and (as a result) the accounting firm they represented were the right ones to do business with, could support the client effectively and communicate on the same wavelength.

The senior partners could relate to the entrepreneur and this was very much in doubt whether the senior managers, to become partners, could do emulate them and do the same. Overall, it was considered that as the senior managers were 'wage slaves', and had not been brought in as equity partners nor perhaps founded the firm they were not hungry enough, did not have the same experience as the entrepreneurs and therefore could not be on the same wavelength as their clients.

This book therefore should enable senior managers to empathise with the ego of the entrepreneur and if not then at least go some way to enable their development.

It has been explained what goes through the entrepreneurs mind, how precious he is about his business but also, in what areas he needs guidance.

The areas are very clear:

- gentle coercion and encouragement in making the entrepreneur's idea and dream become a reality

- support in a professional way to enable the entrepreneur to put in place financial forecasts and budgets to present to financiers to enable the strategy

- constructive criticism, answers and alternatives not negatives

- KPI's which are readily available and simple to interpret for alarm bells to ring

- To give a 'reality check' at times of difficulty.

Any of these can be provided by the senior manager in an accounting firm to the entrepreneur, as the senior manager is adequately qualified in terms of experience and professionalism to see these issues. What they may not have is the experience to sell those ideas and put them across such that the entrepreneur takes them on board, otherwise colloquially known as 'gravitas'.

You can only learn by experience. The entrepreneur is learning on the job and with all the risk, hence the high degree of sensitivity required.

Servicing the entrepreneur can be difficult, they can be demanding and on occasions want matters their own way. It is imperative to explain, albeit difficult, that this is not always possible. The entrepreneur will look at the senior manager as if they are only a senior manager and not an entrepreneur.

While the senior manager is qualified and may become partner, it is a fact that they are not effectively an entrepreneur. This is clearly demonstrated by the experience of someone who has created a firm themselves from scratch and faced the pains of winning customers, servicing customers, employing staff and finding suitable premises as well as kept up with technological developments.

Probably the senior manager is not as equipped as the entrepreneur, but that does not mean they are not able to give good and sound advice. The senior manager must just couch their advice as sensitively as possible.

Seasoned professionals and consultants exist in many professional firms. It is this experience they are offering and not necessarily the same experiences. The entrepreneur needs to understand that and have 'two-way' empathy. The entrepreneur cannot simply seek advice from professionals and always expect the same answer, in fact if they did so they would be limiting their understanding.

Dealing with the entrepreneur may take the form of selling to or supplying their business.

Entrepreneurs like to be respected by others. Any stronger word would do them an injustice.

To sell to the entrepreneur, the seller needs to be strong and committed. These are the traits the entrepreneur has within their own character and needs to see in others.

The supplier must deliver a quality product, on time and at the right price. The entrepreneur would see any failure to do so as a personal affront. The entrepreneur will almost certainly remain loyal to that supplier. Trust wins the day.

In respect of the entrepreneur selling to a customer, he will similarly always almost without exception, commit to achieving the delivery, service levels, price and quality required because it is their name, their firm and most importantly their reputation at stake.

When firms get bigger it is this level of commitment that understandably gets watered down and the firms that win are those with 'legendary service' as mentioned before. The entrepreneur would not let the customer down, it is in his own DNA. Therefore to be supplied by an entrepreneur or an entrepreneurial firm is a delight. Service as you would want and expect, is most evident.

The team managing or working for the business clearly are empowered and motivated as they are trusted with the business. Such values are personally demonstrated by the entrepreneur, if they are still working there, and/or the mission statement and ethos. This message is not necessarily communicated explicitly but the entrepreneur should be employing those with that ethic.

Referring back to deputies or the second in command or those coming through the ranks such as the senior managers, they can become entrepreneurial by displaying those attributes with passion, energy and commitment.

Moving on to those around the entrepreneur, such as fellow board members, this book should give them clear direction and guidance on how to deal with the entrepreneur.

The entrepreneur may be:

- headstrong

- self-opinionated

- set on a journey

- immoveable from certain objectives

- difficult to handle and overly loyal in certain areas

- able to cover up a lack of knowledge and professionalism

- showing a lack of ability in certain key skills.

It is down to the other board members if not the role of the Chairperson or president to be able to manipulate the entrepreneur to understand these weaknesses.

The entrepreneur will have made a bold step in appointing a non-executive Chairperson or president to their organisation, and should be able to listen to their words of wisdom. If not, then the entrepreneur is wasting their time and the time of the non-executive chairperson. The chairperson is also giving their name to the organisation, and of course that of the board.

Board meetings should be the forum to deliver all messages, good, bad and indifferent.

Board meetings should be the place for:

- information to be provided

- papers to be submitted

- decisions to be made

- agendas given on strategy

- assessments on senior key personnel performance

- setting ethos and culture

- the setting of the direction of the business.

The non-executive chairperson has the role of co-ordinating with the entrepreneur, not going off at a tangent even though they may be inclined to.

If the entrepreneur is tangential then it is a weakness not only of the entrepreneur but also the non-executive or executive chairperson, and the board itself, because obviously the entrepreneur is not finding the board meetings worthwhile or necessary.

The chairperson (promoted from non-executive) has to ensure that the board is acting as one. This role among many is where the chairperson must empathise with the entrepreneur.

- The board is the only place of reckoning for the business. There is no-one else who can save the business from itself.

- The decisions made have to be right and timely. Markets entered or strategy made on services offered or products produced have to be 'spot on' or quickly exited.

- The board has to be accountable and understand the investments made and the payback. Profit allows survival.

- The board needs to address how the outside world views the business, the culture and the services on offer. The market perception engages customers and interest.

The board cannot be allowed to wonder:

- Why Albert has not produced the monthly financial statements, when will they be forthcoming and how accurate are they?

- Why Bill, in production, has a company car outside of the existing company policy?

- Why Carol in HR is upsetting everyone with her annual appraisals?

- What colour toilet paper David thinks fits with the company culture?

- Why Elizabeth on reception is always late?

Any board or entrepreneur discussing these at a board meeting has not stepped up to the mark and will always remain a businessperson at that level.

From the above, it is very evident that the entrepreneur has a responsibility to ensure that once the business moves on from giving them a living, they have a duty of care to their employees, customers and suppliers. This is not just their show.

The entrepreneur:

- needs to have empathy with others

- must ensure his ego is managed correctly

- has an awful lot to offer

- must not think they are surrounded by fools

- must not think that every idea is a good one

- must listen

- is key to any business community.

The entrepreneur is a wonderful person and should be treated as such, with great respect. The ability to provide employment, at their risk, is beyond doubt a gift to society and philanthropic, as such.

The entrepreneur owes it to themselves to be honest and by doing so will fulfil their dreams of success.

This humility, awareness and fairness to others will earn respect. It is not all about ego. Vision, drive, passion and judgement are essential ingredients to add to their basic skills and knowledge.

8.4 Backing an entrepreneur

From the above it is clear that the entrepreneur is a different person to most. They have to be.

If you are seeking to support an entrepreneur it seems sensible and logical to first review their business plan, understand that they know their product and their capability and also their market share.

However neither banks, nor venture capital houses, nor business angels carry out any profiling of the entrepreneur with psychometric tests or any form of psychology to understand that they have the required traits to be an entrepreneur and to be entrusted with the capital provided.

This is surely critical to the provision of the seed capital or start finance.

The integrity and responsibility evident in this book is of as great importance as the attitude to measured risk and strategy. The profile is essential.

£££ OUR SURVEY ASKED...

Finally, you have invested £450,000 in to a business for equipment and working capital. The business has made losses to date but due to an increase in sales activity has broken even for the last quarter, which finished only a fortnight ago. However, it is now very clear that the business needs a further cash injection of £50,000. Please read the background issues below:

- The bank will not extend a facility
- You morally cannot ask family or friends to invest (again)
- You are 100% confident that the business will turnaround it just needs time and the further £50,000, as indications are that sales in the past few months have steadily increased each month
- Your spouse is set against the further investment
- You have not taken any income from the business yet
- The £50,000 of savings reduces your joint building society account to nil and your eldest child is excited to move to a fee paying school in three months, just as you feel the business will turn the corner.

If your spouse reluctantly accedes to your request, do you invest this £50,000?

72% said yes they would invest their final £50,000

Within the survey, you will recall that 79% said that they were up to taking risks

Of those,74% said yes to this question and 26% said no

Within the survey, you will recall that 21% said that they were NOT up to taking risks

Of those 59% said yes to this question and 41% said no

26% of the riskier set refused this opportunity when faced with the finality of the decision – nearly 1 in 3, or 20% of the total population surveyed, 1 in 5.

Even with the 'less risky set', 21%, when faced with backing their own judgement, would support this venture. The statistic means an average of 59% would put their last funds in to a venture they were more or less certain would pay back and turn the corner, almost 6 out of 10, or 12% of our total population surveyed, 1 in 8.

These statistics are interesting as they confirm the earlier statistic that 100% back their own judgement. The question outlines a risky situation but one which the entrepreneur can work to their advantage. Hence perhaps polar opposite answers provided – perhaps not what you would expect. You would expect even less of the 'less risky set' refusing the opportunity but materially less than the 1 to 5 or 8.

However, it is comforting to see that of the 79% who said they were risky, that 74% or 3 out of 4 would back themselves and perhaps do so to the detriment of themselves and their family. That is commitment and a responsibility and integrity to see matters through.

This can only truly be measured if the same question was put to employees, considered less risky or risk adverse, who would perhaps say the reverse.

Another key element of the (entrepreneur's) profile to understand must be luck. **Quantify luck?** Luck is where the entrepreneur sees an opportunity and has the resources to act on it. If it is then successful, **that is considered luck.**

They can build a sound enough business case in their mind to see the outcome and deliver it. They have the vision. They take the opportunities presented to them and thereby **maximise their luck**.

Others would not do so.

In summary there are many other elements of the personality that need to be understood. They can be evident in the track record and the demeanour of the person who sets themselves out to be an entrepreneur. But if this is their first venture, then a profile is essential.

Banks generally want some form of security to lend.

Venture capitalists and angels want to identify a good idea to support.

Ordinarily the agreement to the financial support can be down to the entrepreneur that is being backed. Are they fundable? It is the entrepreneur who is being backed financially and supported in whose hands the success of the venture will rest.

£££ OUR SURVEY ASKED...

Your spouse does not agree. You have no choice and do not invest. Do you?

	% answers
Make a concerted effort to make more sales	80%
Struggle on, delaying payments to others	76%
Reduce costs further other than redundancies	67%
Make redundancies	45%
Try to convince your spouse of the merits	43%
Seek an expensive short term loan	16%
Close the business	4%

Our entrepreneur is a hardy character, perhaps now we can summarise and understand their ego in our own minds.

CHAPTER NINE

CONCLUSION

9.1 Closing remarks

This section allows us to reflect on the major character traits of the entrepreneur and what it is within them that will set them apart.

To begin, it is important to understand that unless the landscape in terms of economic stability is evident then no entrepreneur can succeed. Government and enduring social history must be in evidence and without those, in each country there will surface potentially a 'gangster business community' and possibly a 'corrupt officialdom'.

This chapter also includes the survey and bibliography and research.

9.2 Setting the landscape

Any entrepreneur can start and operate their business as long as the jurisdiction and environment where they are operating their business is both politically and economically right. By this, we mean that the country in which they conduct the activity has to have a stable government that will deliver over time and an economy that supports business. As a result the entrepreneurial spirit will develop, be fostered and thrive. Over time most Western democracies have allowed this to happen.

We shall look at three specific examples to illustrate how our entrepreneur cannot operate unless the landscape allows otherwise.

In the UK there was the first industrial revolution and accordingly there has been a stable political and economic environment for over 300 years, based on legislative and democratic structure. The UK has been a world-leading economy and the government provides tax incentives for investment in business, primarily small- to medium-size and start-ups. The EIS and SEIS schemes are the most popular current examples. Investors receive income tax relief on their investment in to a 'qualifying' company under certain restrictions, given certain allowances. If the investor is a higher rate taxpayer then the initial investment in the qualifying company would cost the investor/taxpayer, at the outset, only, say 60%, of the initial down payment as the government effectively gives the tax relief back to the investor on completion of their annual tax assessment form.

Thus, the investment is seen as being cheaper, offering less to lose and the government is seen to be encouraging small business with this incentive.

Small business is collectively the largest 'employer' in the UK economy.

£££ OUR SURVEY ASKED...

Is the first bill that you look to pay government taxes?
52% said yes

Do you save for your government taxes to be able to pay them on time?
72% said yes

Do you consider your tax bills too high?
84% said yes

Do you consider the government incentives and schemes for tax for venture and seed capital such as EIS, SEIS, VCT and the relief on sale such as entrepreneurial relief, good?
52% said yes

That these incentives go far enough?
80% said no

Do you consider legislation for business (employment law/health and safety) are far too onerous against the businessman and complicated?
88% said yes

In your business, do you feel 'weighed down' by bureaucracy?
56% said yes

There are some very salutary statistics within those questions, not least that tax and legislation. While tax and legislation provide the framework to operate and offers essential public services, they are seen as a burden for business. They are generally by far the entrepreneur's biggest cost.

The entrepreneur in the UK copes with this burden.

In Germany during the first few months of the recent financial crisis the demand for luxury products and particularly motor vehicles dropped significantly, such that the German car market lost production to cheaper countries. To achieve cost savings and to stop having excess numbers of highly skilled but unused workers, German car manufacturers laid off the surplus operators.

However the German authorities knew that over time economic cycles change and that the pre-crisis demand would return. If it did so then, unless the workforce could 'upskill' quickly, the new demand would be lost forever to the cheaper countries. The German government took the view that their product quality should stand the test as customers should return when the worldwide economic conditions allowed and the cheaper products with inferior quality would not last and be found wanting compared to the superior German quality and build.

So, unlike the UK where unemployment benefit was provided by the UK government to the unemployed – paid from UK taxes, the German government put in place a scheme to fund the older (say over-50) workers who had been made redundant to attend the production facility or facilities two or three days a week to train younger workers (say under-25) to pass on their knowledge, skill and work ethic. With this in mind the car production would not be lost when demand recovered.

This is a clear and practical insight into the way governments can set a landscape for entrepreneurs to achieve their aims and objectives.

With the BRICs much is being written about and expected by the new world order of economies. Brazil, Russia, India and China are the four major contenders to take on the current G7 of developed, large economies in the world. It is currently estimated that by 2050 these four countries will be alongside the USA and Japan as the leading six economies in the new world order, to be closely followed by the UK, Germany, France and Italy.

The reason being put forward is that they have the population and therefore the consumption and demand, the recent growth and the future expected growth, the right exchange rate and therefore the ability to export cheaply. The only item missing with them all, to create a realistic chance of fulfilling this expectation, is the political order and legislative backdrop.

Each and every one of these four countries could have a major draw-back during the next 30 years that may prevent development of a sustainable economy in the new world order.

Brazil has regularly had a change of government up to the end of the 20th century and the most recent has made inflation targeting its priority, providing Brazil with the respect it demands in the world order. However political unrest could arise at any moment while the country acclimatises itself to its new economic panacea. This could stop any development and disenfranchise any entrepreneur in that country to operate successfully.

Russia's political classes and governing regime, which is not based on any Western ideals, contains corrupt governance and poor legal structures. This itself can halt it as it strides towards growth needed to make it a major economic player and the resulting entrepreneurial spirit for many, not just the few.

India is challenged by its ability to control the ever-growing numbers of its population and the demands that that places on the economy in terms of health care and public services and stopping poverty. Poverty in the masses while creating demand can stifle the economy and India has its future in its own hands. Its literacy is poor compared to other major economies. Currently about 20% of children between six and 14 do not attend school. This social policy needs understanding and then rectifying to allow the economic stability needed for the entrepreneur to flourish.

China itself probably has the best chance of succeeding however it is a communist society. It is one where the entrepreneurial spirit and political regime may clash rather than harmonise. Many Chinese have moved to cities, allowing demand to soar. The renminbi is heavily backed to take over from the dollar as the world reserve currency but the pollution in the cities, the potential for inflation and the Communist party, being itself the largest political party in the world and also the largest chamber of commerce, may restrict the spirit required for entrepreneurs to succeed.

These issues may well hamper the development of this otherwise reasonably stable domain. Such stability is why China is currently succeeding and being seen as a model new economy. Growth rates are attractive compared to the low percentages being achieved in the developed Western world. China is a source of much admiration at this time.

From these examples of government intervention or support it is very clear that to succeed, the entrepreneur needs the structure of governance and 'history' to provide:

- a good and sound banking system,

- a stable and supportive regime of taxation and public services

- the potential for local demand,

- policies to control inflation,

- an exchange-rate policy which does not fluctuate wildly,

- a history of political stability for attracting inward investment.

Industrialisation across public-sector services such that the population will be cared for, supported and allowed to thrive and that social unrest, corruption and crime are kept to a minimum. **This emanates as an elected government not a political doctrine.**

After the BRICs there are a 'next 11', with the acronym N-11. The countries are spread across the world being, in no particular order: Egypt, Iran, Mexico, Nigeria and Turkey and six countries from Asia: Bangladesh, Indonesia, Korea, Pakistan, the Philippines and Vietnam.

This is not a history lesson or a political debate, but the success of those countries to develop and pull more people out of poverty and into the consuming middle classes to facilitate greater trade and wealth creation will be based on overcoming the obstacles of political turmoil and unstable government.

To review their political status 10, 20 and 50 years from now will determine how the local entrepreneur will survive within each country and, by default, foreign entrepreneurs dealing within each country.

Stable government and incentives for the entrepreneur are critical and essential ingredients of the landscape within which they need to operate. It is clear why the entrepreneur has succeeded in Western countries such as the UK and USA.

9.3 The major characteristics possessed by an entrepreneur

From reading the previous chapters we can summarise the character of an entrepreneur.

- **The primary attributes are passion, energy and charisma.**

The entrepreneur possesses these in abundance. The passion for an idea, product and/or business allows them to have the energy to take it forward from inception to finish, where others may fail or give up. This energy could be likened to foolishness if they are unsuccessful and perhaps even over optimism but anyone setting up a business must possess these attributes together with the necessary time to attend to the business.

Passion without the time and the attention is worthless. Unnecessary demands on time and any negative energy will sap their will to succeed.

The entrepreneur, as a business leader, will also have charisma. They need this to lead and motivate their team and those around them. Those that supply them or most importantly to whom they sell, will enjoy and empathise with their charisma such that they will want to work for, supply to and buy from the entrepreneur.

It will be a pleasurable relationship.

There must be a belief that everyone involved in the process of the business is equally important. That everyone will win and succeed by being involved with the activity. Support the charismatic, passionate and highly energised person and success will follow them and those around them.

These attributes go hand-in-hand with the self-belief, exampled by 100% of our survey stating that the entrepreneur backed their own judgement when making decisions.

- **The second important set of noticeable attributes would be vision, strategic thinking and the ability to take opportunities.**

Vision is something that people rarely possess. Vision can be linked to self-confidence.

Vision is the ability to see ahead, to see what is in store. Vision is having an analytical brain and envisaging a critical path that may occur in the future, setting it out for others to follow and be able to adhere to it. This enables any variances to be dealt with and put in perspective, such that the business itself in its entirety is not jeopardised. The facility to create 'what if' analyses in the mind not necessarily always on paper helps so that the business can plan and cope with unexpected turns of event.

This leads us to strategic thinking and planning. Unless the entrepreneur is thinking ahead, planning and strategically thinking, then the business will not be able to take full advantage of opportunities as they are presented. It will meander.

A strategy is vital. When setting out on a journey you look at the map, not only to understand how you are undertaking the journey but also the time it will take.

The mini milestones towards a major milestone or achievement are critical. During this journey opportunities are presented and can be taken – or not.

The taking of an opportunity and the strategic thinking to resource the opportunity to make it a success is the closest we shall get to analysing the luck that 96% of our survey considered to be so critical to the entrepreneur's success.

Not taking some opportunities as they are presented is equally as important. To take the right opportunities is critical. So the ability to recognise the right opportunity is down to careful analysis and perhaps intuition, which plays the part in their 'luck'.

- **The third set of (outwardly visible) attributes for the entrepreneur to possess are a clear focus, sheer hard work and lots of drive.**

Entrepreneurs set themselves jobs to do and do them.

They are achievers, completers and finishers.

They have a clear focus and not withstanding anything dramatic or traumatic they will achieve that goal or aim, generally within the set, allotted timescale. This is focus. It is achieved by hard work. Not just putting in hours, but spending time working effectively and efficiently such that the time they spend on any project, problem or task is less than another would.

Not much stands in their way to fulfil the project. They don't fall ill.

Hard work can be measured by output. Meetings attended, reports written, sales made. The entrepreneur will score very heavily on all of these. Most entrepreneurs will also excel or do well at a number of activities. They are multi-talented individuals so they may well perform well at sports, arts or other non-work activities. This is because they will concentrate on an activity in hand and attempt to do it well or to the best of their ability. This gives, by default, the entrepreneur a greater depth of personality and they are therefore interesting people with which to engage.

Drive is the key to success, not to take 'no' as an answer, and achieve the end game which has been set. The driven entrepreneur will get up at 5am and get to the early morning meeting miles away from home or will stay late to finish a report and/or work on the Sunday to get Monday off to a flying start. The driven entrepreneur will not make excuses. Every email will be answered and dealt with in a timely fashion. They are known as 'doers'.

These visual and highly perceptible characteristics make the entrepreneur the exciting person they are.

However there are two more sets of attributes or abilities that could be considered as being internal or inward looking.

They are:

- **being highly organised, very responsible and, much more often than perhaps thought, operates responsibly towards others.**

Any businessperson has to be organised. They have to achieve to get results.

They have to deliver and this can only be done by knowing and listing the requirements, setting priorities and doing these in a fashion such that they are effectively completed. Not half done or left.

The organisation of individual roles and responsibilities allows time for achieving the right thing right, 'doing' rather than 'saying'.

The entrepreneur will have an organised mind, a tidy desk and a clear in-tray which means that every piece of post, email, or output is effective and to the point.

The successful entrepreneur will make lists and cross out everything achieved. They will then make a new list and so on.

An organised businessperson is both efficient and hard-working. This can be to the extent of being obsessive, which can be quite understandable and often taken to an extreme as the entrepreneur will take it personally if anything is left undone or the subject of lateness or complaint. A successful entrepreneur may be seen late at night or early in the morning doing menial tasks, just to get them done.

The obsession will not be understood by co-workers, perhaps admired, but not clearly understood. However, the obsession, while not a disorder is a differentiating factor. An obsessive personality is often seen as a disorder and that may well be but it is, on this occasion, turned into a benefit as it effectively means they leave no stone unturned.

The entrepreneur is clearly responsible.

They will pay their taxes, generally on time, they will pay suppliers and most importantly staff.

Any businessman who thinks that is a way of making more money by cheating the government purse or at worse others does not understand protocol as they would certainly not want it done to them. Integrity and responsibility is a key factor to a successful entrepreneur demonstrating a complete and rounded character.

Integrity is an attractive attribute and adds to charisma. Dealing with people properly commands loyalty and above all trust.

- **A further, fifth and last set of attributes are those relating to an internal ability in logic and mathematics.**

The entrepreneur has to understand what the process has to be to deliver and to deliver at a profit.

They have to understand the critical path to create a supply chain to the customer, in a logical and clear way. They have to communicate that easily to those around them. If they are unclear on the numbers, being sales, break-even analyses and profits then they will, in time, fail.

A great sign of 'intelligence' (as we know it) for the entrepreneur is to be mathematical, if not highly mathematical, such that mental arithmetic is second nature.

If this does not come naturally then the entrepreneur should train in this area. This would be the only trait that may not come naturally.

We have assumed that the entrepreneur knows their market and/or is technically very proficient in the area in which they operate.

These internal sets of attributes make the entrepreneur a 'deeper' and much more measured person than first thought.

So overall, the five sets of attributes above, which themselves contain three words each, can be supported and summarised by **one word for each set, resulting in five key words.** They could be labelled a '7th sense' and, of course, are the skill set and character of the successful entrepreneur.

Vigorous

(from passion, energy and charisma)

Intuitive

(creating own luck) (from vision, strategy and opportunity)

Strong-minded

(from focus, hard work and drive)

Ordered

(from organisation, responsibility and integrity)

Reasoned

(from logic and mathematics)

Any backer or investor should profile their target investment and understand the 'manager', soon to become entrepreneur, who they are backing.

There seems little point wasting time and money in a venture that does not have the correct 'captain' or 'captaincy' at the helm.

Entrepreneurs are a breed. Psychologists should surely be able to devise a test to enable this profiling.

Entrepreneurs have a major role to play in society and the advancement of society through them should be treated and welcomed as such.

Governments wishing to develop their industrial base and grow their economies should incentivise their own class of entrepreneur within each country.

Not everyone can be an entrepreneur, **it suits only some.**

As you relate and deal with an entrepreneur, you do need to **empathise with the ego of the entrepreneur.**

£££ OUR SURVEY ASKED...
Is there another skill required for the successful entrepreneur?

A sample of pertinent answers were:
- Recognising potential and investing in your own potential
- Balancing all the skills required
- Creating a great team
- Man management and motivation
- Adaptability
- Understanding others
- Coping and dealing with the 'hits'

This is food for thought.

9.4 The survey

The survey we sent to a sample of entrepreneurs is below. Please complete it yourself and see where you fit and how you score.

1. Please mark the following characteristics in order of importance (1-7), that you feel most define an entrepreneur?

    1 being the least important and 7 being the most important

Courage	
Leadership quality (ie character)	
Hungry/needs must (ie rags to riches)	
Free thinking	
Inventive/Creative	
Hardworking/Driven	
Risk taking	

2. Is there another characteristic that needs mentioning?

3.   Out of 10, please mark the following characteristics that are required in the 'make up' of an entrepreneur?

1 is not required and 10 is certainly required

Bombastic	
Ruthless	
Can make the really tough decisions	
Extrovert	
Single minded	
Strategic thinker	
Does not suffer fools	

4.   Is there another requirement that is missing here, if so please highlight it below?

5.   Do you feel that successful entrepreneurs stick to what they know?

(please mark your answer)

Yes	No

6. Do you feel that, in general, a previous business failure helps an entrepreneur succeed?

(please mark your answer)

Yes	No

7. Do you feel that the fear of failure drives an entrepreneur?

(please mark your answer)

Yes	No

8. Please mark in order (1-6), what you think is the main cause for businesses to fail?

1 being the least important cause and 6 being the most important

Insufficient financial information	
Insufficient capital and finance	
Recession and outside forces	
Owner's excessive drawings	
Failure to pay government taxes	
Lack of strategic direction	

9. Is there another reason, in your view, that businesses may fail?

10. Was a parent an entrepreneur or businessperson?

   (please mark your answer)

Yes	No

11. Did you start with?

   (please mark your answer)

Your own money	Yes	No
Friends and family money	Yes	No
Bank funding	Yes	No
Venture capital	Yes	No
No money	Yes	No
Other	Yes	No

12. Have you set yourself identifiable milestones to achieve?

    (please mark your answer)

Yes	No

13. If yes, and if you have achieved that first milestone did you immediately present yourself with another?

    (please mark your answer)

N/A	Yes	No

14. What are your first 3 milestones? (If you haven't set them, set them now)

    Mark 3 of the above in order, 3 being the first and 1 the last

A sales figure	3	2	1
A profit figure	3	2	1
To earn a living	3	2	1
To repay seed capital	3	2	1
To increase your net worth	3	2	1
To prove you could do it to yourself	3	2	1
To prove you could do it to others	3	2	1

15. What level of education do you have?

(please mark your answer)

No external exams	Yes	No
O level/GCSE	Yes	No
A level	Yes	No
HND or other	Yes	No
Degree	Yes	No
Masters	Yes	No
Professional qualification	Yes	No
Other	Yes	No

16. Do you think that a formal education to degree level is important for entrepreneurs?

(please mark your answer)

Yes	No

17. Do you think that while a formal education may not be important that some selling experience in the work environment, at least, is important?

   (please mark your answer)

Yes	No

18. Please order (1-5) the skills below in importance for an entrepreneur?

   1 being the least important and 5 being the most important

Marketing	
Sales	
Operational processes	
Finance	
Inventiveness and creativity (R&D)	

19. Is there another skill required for the successful entrepreneur?

20. It is considered that there are various forms of intelligence. These are marked below. Please rate these in order of importance (1-7) for an entrepreneur and how relevant they are (1-10) to the skill set of an entrepreneur?

1 being the least important and 7 being the most important
In respect of relevance 1 being irrelevant and 10 being essential

Logical and mathematical	Yes	No		
Inter personal (relationships)	Yes	No		
Intra personal (you know yourself)	Yes	No		
Linguistic	Yes	No		
Spatial	Yes	No		
Bodily kinaesthetic	Yes	No		
Musical	Yes	No		

21. Do you consider you have had some luck? If so please mark its importance to you to where you are now, out of 10, if not lucky then mark under 5.

(please mark your answer)

Luck	Yes	No	

22. Do you consider you have been in the right place at the right time? If so please mark its importance to you to where you are now, out of 10, if not then mark under 5.

(please mark your answer)

Right place at right time	Yes	No	

23. Do you consider you are in the right sector? If so please mark its importance to you to where you are now, out of 10, if not then mark under 5.

(please mark your answer)

Right sector	Yes	No	

24. Do you think you take risks? If so please mark how 'risky' you think you are, out of 10. If risk adverse mark below 5.

(please mark your answer)

Taking risks	Yes	No	

25. Rather than taking risks, do you back your own judgement? If so, then please mark out of 10 how confident you are of your own ability.

(please mark your answer)

Taking risks	Yes	No	

26. Do you generally discuss big decisions with others, as a sounding board?

(please mark your answer)

Yes	No

27. Please answer the following?

(please mark your answer)

Have you considered employing a Chairman?	Yes	No
Do you employ a Chairman?	Yes	No
Do you wish you had more finance in the business?	Yes	No
Have you sought external finance?	Yes	No
Do you recognise any weaknesses in yourself?	Yes	No
Have you compensated for those weaknesses?	Yes	No

28. Is there a skill base missing within your business, if so would you or have you recruited to fill that skill base?

(please mark your answer)

Selling	Yes	No
Marketing	Yes	No
Wider industry knowledge	Yes	No
Operations	Yes	No
Finance	Yes	No
Research and development, inventiveness	Yes	No
You cover it all	Yes	No

29. What has made you successful?

30. Do you read management books?

(please mark your answer)

Yes	No

31. Do you go on courses to develop yourself, your skill set and self-educate?

(please mark your answer)

Yes	No

32. Do you have an overall strategy and if so how important is it to keep to it? If you have answered yes, your score should be 10 for it to be very important.

(please mark your answer)

Overall strategy	Yes	No	

33. Do you have a niche service or product and if so, how important is it to keep to it? If you have answered yes, your score should be 10 for it to be very important

(please mark your answer)

Niche service or product	Yes	No	

34. Have you or do you try other services or products and if so, how important is it for them to succeed? If you have answered yes, your score should be 10 for it to be very important.

(please mark your answer)

Other services or products	Yes	No

35. Do you have key performance indicators in your business?

(please mark your answer)

Daily	Yes	No
Weekly	Yes	No
Monthly	Yes	No
Never - wait for the year end	Yes	No
One important one provided at various intervals	Yes	No

36. Do you have an exit strategy?

(please mark your answer)

Yes	No

37. At what age?

Did you want your own business	
Did you start your first business	
Did you consider yourself successful	
Do you wish to retire (not exit this business)	

38. Do you?

(please mark your answer)

Spend more time than you feel you should on this business	Yes	No
Feel that you do not have a work/life balance	Yes	No
Feel pleased that you spend so much time on the business	Yes	No
Engage regularly in a pastime outside of work	Yes	No
Exercise regularly (2 or 3 times a week)	Yes	No
Feel guilty that you are away from your family	Yes	No
Take more than 20 days off a year as holiday	Yes	No
Have you been divorced	Yes	No
If so, do you feel the business was a major contributory factor	Yes	No

39. Many entrepreneurs are successful and have the trappings of wealth, can you answer the following?

(please mark your answer)

Have you had an addiction*?	Yes	No
Have you ever felt self-indulgent?	Yes	No
Have you consulted a therapist for anything?	Yes	No
Do you feel others are clearly jealous of you?	Yes	No
If yes, do you feel they understand the cost to you of being an entrepreneur?	Yes	No
Do you feel that life would be easier if you had not got your own business?	Yes	No
Do you like the trappings of success?	Yes	No
Do you aspire to more success and more trappings?	Yes	No
Do you try to hide your wealth?	Yes	No

*An addiction may be related to: alcohol, drugs, smoking, spending, eating, sex or even spending an excessive time on a pastime.

40. You have decided that there is ample spare cash in the business to draw for yourself. Your passion is sailing. You have always yearned for a particular boat. Do you?

(please mark your answer, only one choice)

Buy that boat or small yacht	Yes	No
Put the same amount in to a pension fund	Yes	No
Buy an investment property with a better than expected return	Yes	No
Give bonuses to key staff	Yes	No
Keep the money in the bank	Yes	No
Fund a friends 'start up' business, with appropriate tax relief	Yes	No

41. You decide that you can draw, but not as much as above. Do you?

(please mark your answer, choose your first (1) and second (2) priorities)

Pay off as much of your debt as you can	1	2	No
Treat the family to the holiday of a lifetime	1	2	No
Buy an expensive car	1	2	No
Put a deposit down for an investment property	1	2	No
Give smaller bonuses to key staff	1	2	No
Keep the money in the bank	1	2	No
Fund your pension	1	2	No

42. Having drawn the amount above and fulfilled your immediate and your family's dreams and wishes you develop a philanthropic and social conscience and wish to give to charity? What percentage of the amount in Question 39 do you give?

(please mark your answer)

None	Under 10%	Under 50%	Under 75%	Under 100%	Over 100%

43. Is the first bill that you look to pay government taxes?

(please mark your answer)

Yes	No

44. Do you save for your government taxes to be able to pay them on time?

(please mark your answer)

Yes	No

45. Do you consider all your tax bills (overall) too high?

(please mark your answer)

Yes	No

46. Do you consider the government incentives and schemes for tax for venture and seed capital such as EIS, SEIS, VCT and the relief on sale such as entrepreneurial relief......good?

(please mark your answer)

Yes	No

47. That these incentives go far enough?

(please mark your answer)

Yes	No

48. Do you consider legislation for business (Employment Law/ Health and Safety) are far too onerous **against** the businessman and complicated?

(please mark your answer)

Yes	No

49. In your business, do you feel 'weighed down' by bureaucracy?

(please mark your answer)

Yes	No

50. Finally, you have invested £450,000 into a business for equipment and working capital. The business has made losses to date but due to an increase in sales activity has broken even for the last quarter, which finished only a fortnight ago. However, it is now very clear that the business needs a further cash injection of £50,000. Please read the background issues below:

- The bank will not extend a facility

- You morally cannot ask family or friends to invest (again)

- You are 100% confident that the business will turnaround it just needs time and the further £50,000, as indications are that sales in the last few months have steadily increased each month

- Your spouse is set against the further investment

- You have not taken any income from the business yet

- The £50,000 of savings reduces your joint building society account to nil and your eldest child is excited to move to a fee paying school in three months, just as you feel the business will turn the corner.

If your spouse reluctantly accedes to your request, do you invest this £50,000?

(please mark your answer)

Yes	No

Your spouse does not agree. You have no choice and do not invest. Do you?

(please mark your answer, being any or all of these)

Close the business	Yes	No
Struggle on, delaying payments to creditors	Yes	No
Seek an expensive short term loan	Yes	No
Make redundancies	Yes	No
Make more of a concerted effort to increase sales	Yes	No
Reduce costs yet further other than redundancies	Yes	No
Try to convince your spouse of the merits	Yes	No

9.5 Bibliography

- Manias, Panics and Crashes - A history of financial crises
  By Charles P Kindleberger and Robert Z Aliber

- Outliers
  By Malcolm Gladwell

- The Ragged Trousered Philanthropists
  By Robert Tressell

- The Sunday Times Rich List
- The New Statesman Magazine
- The Times literary Supplement
- Original research by Howard Gardner on the multiple forms of intelligence
- Original research by Dr Meredith Belbin on team roles